Instructor's Resource Manual
to accompany

INDUSTRIAL/ ORGANIZATIONAL PSYCHOLOGY

Understanding the Workplace   Fifth Edition

Paul E. Levy
The University of Akron

Kristie Campana
Minnesota State University—Mankato

worth publishers
Macmillan Learning

New York

I/O Psychology: Then and Now

LEARNING OBJECTIVES

This chapter should help students understand:

- How I/O psychologists are trained
- The work of I/O psychologists and how it benefits organizations and employees alike
- The diverse historical trends associated with the development and growth of I/O psychology
- The very important role currently being played by I/O psychology in the changing workplace, as well as the field's great potential to contribute to organizational functioning in the future

Chapter Summary

I/O psychology, the application of psychology to the workplace, encompasses such diverse areas as performance appraisal, employment testing, organizational development, and motivation. I/O psychologists receive extensive training in a wide range of areas, but their central approach is based on the scientist/practitioner model, which emphasizes both theory and practice. Most obtain an advanced degree such as a PhD. The training is quite intensive and includes a great deal of coursework, practical experience, and research experience. The culmination of the training is usually the completion of a dissertation.

Over 40% of I/O psychologists work in academic settings such as psychology departments and business schools, where they teach undergraduate and graduate students and conduct research for the purposes of creating and applying knowledge. The majority of I/O psychologists, however, work outside of academia in the public or private sector, applying what they've learned in graduate school to their particular organization. Many of these I/O psychologists also work for consulting firms that provide services to organizations on a project-by-project basis.

I/O psychology has a rich, albeit relatively short, history. Although its beginnings date to around the turn of the 20th century, its growth as a field emerged with World War I, when I/O psychologists were employed by the government to train, test, and measure the performance of soldiers. Other historical hallmarks include

World War II, the civil rights movement of the 1960s, the emergence of the global economy in the 2000s, and now the technical revolution of the past 15 years. I/O psychology is positioned to play an ever-increasing role in the constantly changing world of work in the 21st century. In the remainder of this book, we will discuss the various topics and areas in which I/O psychology has, and will continue to have, an impact. You should find a great deal of material that you can apply to your life as a student or employee—the applications of I/O psychology are many, diverse, and useful.

TEACHING THE CHAPTER

Similar to the instruction of any course, the first few class periods are critical for establishing student expectations regarding the quality of course instruction and the level of participation expected, as well as the instructor's ability to convey important concepts in a clear, organized, and entertaining way. With this first chapter, it is very important to lay the foundation on which to build students' knowledge of I/O psychology and to foster a positive classroom environment in which exploration and inquiry are promoted.

Therefore, it is recommended that you supplement the administrative tasks on the first day of class with the ice breaker exercise suggested below (or a similar exercise of your own choosing). The formal terminology of numerous I/O topics will likely be new to your students; however, many of them will have had some work experience with most of the topics addressed in this book. Helping them apply their experiences to bring I/O psychology to life is an important first step in making this class an enlightening, relevant, and worthwhile learning experience.

This chapter outlines many of the important milestones during the last 100 years that have contributed to the growth of I/O psychology. In addition, it offers a preliminary introduction to some of the important topics covered later in the book. Topics such as performance appraisal, training, and selection might be completely new to students, but introducing them and explaining how I/O psychologists have been specially trained to work in these areas of organizational life will help students understand what I/O psychology is all about.

Websites are listed later in this chapter to facilitate web-based classroom environments and to supplement the chapter material. These websites can also be incorporated into assignments in which students can explore the sites and create brief reports about the information they have learned. The SIOP and Academy of Management websites contain helpful resources to facilitate student learning. Some *HR Magazine* articles that are frequently relevant to course topics can be viewed on the Society of Human Resource Management website. Illustrating the relevance of I/O psychology to issues in the popular press is a very powerful way of reinforcing the concepts and principles that students will learn in this class.

SUGGESTED EXERCISES AND ASSIGNMENTS

Ice Breaker

Purpose The main objective of this exercise is to introduce students to one another and to the larger class. It will also identify and form class teams that will meet during class time throughout the semester. These teams can engage in discussion of class topics or work on in-class exercises.

Instructions Ask students to pair up with someone they did not know prior to coming to class. Each pair should then introduce themselves to each other. Inform students that they will be responsible for introducing their classmate to the rest of the class in about 5 to 10 minutes. Ask students to gather the following information about each other:

- First name
- Hometown
- Year in school
- Major
- Why they are taking this class
- Best job they have had and why it was the best
- Worst job they have had and why it was the worst

After 5 to 10 minutes have passed, ask partners to introduce each other to you and to the rest of the class. If your class has more than 20 students, this exercise could extend beyond a single class period. Thus, you may want to consider (1) placing a time limit on partner introductions or (2) forming groups of pairs and having each pair introduce each other in the smaller group.

To extend this activity (if time permits), have pairs form into larger groups (four to eight students) and assign each group an I/O topic that will be discussed later in the book (e.g., interviews, training, motivation, recruitment). Give groups 10 to 20 minutes to discuss the following questions with regard to their topic and ask them to present their ideas at the end of the time period:

- How would you define this topic?
- What work experiences have group members (or others they know) had that are relevant to this topic?
- What are examples of good practices regarding this topic?
- What are examples of bad practices regarding this topic? What do they believe could have been done differently by the organization?

I/O Taboo

I/O Taboo is a simple, yet fun, game that can be played in class (facilitated by the instructor) and used as a learning tool for students to study and review important concepts and key words. Students may also be encouraged to play this game with other students outside of class in preparation for exams.

The object of the game is for a team member to get his/her team to say the I/O word (in **bold type** in the following example) by giving clues about the word without mentioning the other words on the card—they are "taboo." One member of the opposing team referees the clues given by the clue-giving team to ensure that the team does not earn points if a taboo word is spoken. As the clue-givers provide clues, their teammates should shout out what they think the I/O word is until they guess it correctly.

Example I/O Taboo game cards are shown below. Using the Key Terms from each chapter of this book, you can create your own game cards with words most relevant to each chapter's topics and to your own lectures.

CHAPTER 1: Example I/O Taboo Cards

Organizational Psychology	Scientist/Practitioner Model	Dissertation
"O" Side Motivation Work Attitudes Groups	Graduate Training SIOP Knowledge Consumers	PhD Research Graduate School Literature Review

I/O Syllabus Hunt

This activity can be used to help students become acquainted with the textbook, the syllabus, or both. Have students form small groups (two to three students) and come up with a problem they have encountered in the workplace. Once they have described the problem, have them look at the book or your syllabus and discuss where they believe they might find a solution to this problem. In smaller classes, you might have groups compete against one another to see who can most quickly find the chapter or class period that sounds most relevant to the problem. Ask students to share some examples so that classmates can begin to think about problems they might be able to solve after completing the course.

SIOP Scavenger Hunt

Purpose Students will have an opportunity to review http://www.siop.org, a useful resource for I/O psychologists and interested students.

Instructions Provide students with computers that have access to the Internet. If you are limited in the number of computers, students can participate in teams. Ask them to use the website to find the following:

- a company that is currently hiring someone with a PhD in I/O psychology.
- a school that offers a master's degree in I/O psychology.
- when and where the next SIOP conference is.
- a consultant who works in your state (or a neighboring state).
- when the graduate student scholarship application materials are due.
- the latest edition of *TIP* (the official SIOP publication).

The group that finds all of this information first wins.

What Topic is Most Interesting?

Purpose Students will be able to discuss what they have read in the book and consider which topics they might find most interesting in the course.

Instructions In the book, it is mentioned that there are five major areas where an I/O psychologist is apt to spend his/her time: selection, training/development, organizational development, performance appraisal, and quality of work life. Ask students to discuss which of these topics they find most interesting and/or important. You may wish to use the following discussion prompts:

- Why do you believe this particular topic is so important?
- How do your own personal experiences with work affect your opinion?
- What outcomes do you think these topics might affect (e.g., motivation, performance)?
- How do you think this topic might change in the 21st century?

EVALUATING "TAKING IT TO THE FIELD"

In this chapter, the "Taking it to the Field" activity asks students to explain what an I/O psychology firm does and how it might help Chris, the CEO of RainCloud, a tech startup, whose company has experienced fast growth recently. There are many possible responses to the scenario, but the points below are suggestions for what poor, good, and excellent responses should look like.

Poor responses…	
	- Contain spelling and grammatical errors, which will not impress a potential client.
	- Fail to explain I/O psychology OR use complex terminology that a layperson would not understand.
	- Do not address the specific problems Chris is experiencing at his company.
	- Are too short to be helpful OR are very long-winded.
	- Are missing a salutation (e.g., "Hello, Chris").
	- Are missing a sign-off (e.g., "Looking forward to speaking with you more! Susan").
Good responses…	
	- Use proper spelling and grammar.
	- Explain what I/O psychology is in a relatively concise and straightforward manner.
	- Have some vague suggestions for Chris's specific problems (e.g., "Maybe you need to do more training with your employees?").
	- May be slightly wordy or a little bit too sparse but nonetheless get the main idea across and demonstrate understanding of the chapter.
	- Should have a salutation.
	- Should have a sign-off.

Excellent responses...
- Use flawless spelling and grammar.
- Provide a short, pithy statement about what topics are encompassed by I/O psychology; a description that goes beyond what Chris mentions as problems can help open the door for future work with him.
- Specifically address how they might help Chris with his problem in a way that shows they have paid attention to the chapter and perhaps have looked at the topics in the table of contents. Students might mention finding ways to more quickly deliver training and development. They may also indicate problems with motivation or leadership within the company. Students should not go into too much depth in their suggestions.
- Should suggest a follow-up meeting or phone call so that they can start working with Chris and coming up with a solution to the problem.
- Contain a salutation.
- Contain a sign-off.

EVALUATING "APPLICATION QUESTIONS"

1. Go to http://www.siop.org and find a university that offers an MA, a PsyD, or a PhD in I/O psychology. Visit that university's I/O psychology page and read about the program. What are some aspects of that program that seem appealing to you? What aspects seem unappealing? If you wanted to apply to this school, what would you need to do?

   Evaluation Guide: Students rarely have a good sense of how to evaluate different programs for graduate training. Here are some suggestions for providing feedback or prompting discussion:

   - If students focus on superficial aspects of the website ("The website looks nice"), you can prompt them to think carefully about what this says about a school: Does a nice-looking website indicate anything about what they will learn or whether they will enjoy what they are learning?
   - If students say things that make it clear they do not understand what graduate training is like ("This program looks too hard!"), you can provide them with a more realistic preview of graduate school and the demands that are involved. You may also share helpful resources for learning about graduate training, such as Robert Peters's excellent book *Getting What You Came For*.
   - If students focus on aspects of the program itself, encourage them to think of different aspects of the program that might be indicators of quality (e.g., what classes they will take, student satisfaction, graduation or placement rates).
   - Students often do not realize the importance of there being a faculty member who is conducting research they find interesting. Encourage them to look

at faculty profiles to see what types of research they might be doing if they attend that school.

2. The chapter mentions five main topics that I/O psychologists investigate— selection, training, organizational development, performance appraisal, and quality of work life. Which of these topics seems most interesting to you? Write a question about that topic that you think I/O psychology could answer.

Evaluation Guide: This activity serves two purposes. First, it allows students to imagine themselves in the role of an I/O psychologist and to seriously consider what types of issues interest them. Second, it allows for a discussion of what questions are appropriate in terms of scientific investigation. Here are some suggestions for providing feedback or prompting discussion:

- If a student brings up a question that is not testable because it deals with opinion rather than fact ("Men are better leaders than women"), you can discuss the importance of being objective and specific in science, emphasizing the need to ask questions that can be answered. You can also guide the student in changing the question so that it is testable ("Men tend to work longer hours than women").

- A student might bring up a question that fits under a different topic than he/she has indicated or that fits under two topics ("Does a webinar actually improve performance?"). You can use this situation to discuss how many questions in I/O psychology bridge different topic areas and how it is helpful for an I/O psychologist to know about many different areas so he/she can be prepared to investigate a number of different questions.

- A student might bring up a question that also connects with a different area of psychology ("What prejudices do African Americans face at work" might also connect to social psychology). You can use this situation to indicate that I/O psychology often uses theories that have been developed in other fields of psychology or business to answer new questions.

3. The chapter discusses the importance of understanding diversity in the workplace. One currently popular topic is the issue of generational differences. How does your attitude toward work differ from that of people who are older or younger than you (e.g., your parents or children)? What kinds of problems might arise out of those differences?

Evaluation Guide: Students tend to be particularly interested in this topic because it is a fairly common topic in the popular media. Students may hone in on a number of stereotypes or generalizations they have heard about their own generation; they may be interested in a discussion of why these generalizations occur and what some consequences of the generalizations might be.

- Younger generations are often stereotyped as feeling entitled as well as being impatient or spoiled. If a student brings up this point, you can discuss differences in how the generations were raised and behaviors of younger people (e.g., not using proper titles like Mr. or Ms.; texting during meetings) that might lead to these perceptions.

- Younger students may also mention that they have different expectations about their work environment (e.g., more flexible work schedules, telecommuting). You might discuss differences between more traditional work environments and changes that are occurring due to new technology. You might also discuss ways that technology can change the way we think and work (e.g., younger students tend to rely on their memory less because it is easy to look up information if it is forgotten; prior to search engines, however, forgetting information cost workers a lot of time).
- Students may also bring up their own negative generalizations about older workers (e.g., crabby, traditional, resistant to change). This can provide an opportunity to discuss some of the problems they might encounter because of these generalizations (e.g., if they come up with an idea, they may need to persuade others to buy into the idea rather than having it adopted immediately).

4. The chapter discusses the role that I/O psychology has to play in helping organizations operate in an ethical manner. Consider a current legal battle in the news today, such as a lawsuit or Supreme Court case involving employee rights, affirmative action, or discrimination; a legislative debate on paid leave, fair compensation, or worker rights and safety; or some other newsworthy development. Based on what you've read in this chapter regarding the work of I/O psychology, how would you as a researcher or practitioner address this issue?

   Evaluation Guide: Student responses will vary. However, the following might be possibilities:
   - I/O psychologists must both meet the requests of their clients and respect the dignity of people they work with. There are many news stories about workers being exploited, manipulated, or unfairly treated. This can be a jumping point to discuss some of the competing pressures I/O psychologists face in their work.
   - I/O psychologists often serve as experts. They can be resources in the workplace (even when the issue at hand is not directly part of their job, such as offering coworkers advice on leadership) in courtrooms (as expert witnesses), and in communities (e.g., I/O psychologists might have good ideas for how to help immigrants update their resumes to get their first job). Students may benefit from discussing how I/O psychologists can use their expertise to help people other than employees in the workplace.
   - I/O psychologists can also play an important role in educating others, including students (as well as I/O professors), employees, and regular citizens. Talk about what I/O psychologists might be able to teach others about affirmative action and diversity in the workplace, worker rights, illegal interview questions, or other areas that may help people navigate the workplace.

5. Consider a problem that you are facing either at work or at school. How might I/O psychology be able to help you solve this problem?

Evaluation Guide: Students can come up with a variety of answers. Some common examples might include the following:

- Arguments or difficulties with roommates (I/O psychology can help you communicate better or select better roommates)
- Having problems getting others to go along with ideas or plans (I/O psychology can help you learn to lead or persuade other people)
- Getting other people to contribute more on class projects or housework (I/O psychology can teach you about how to get teams to work together effectively, how to motivate other people to do tasks, or how to organize work more effectively)
- Feeling dissatisfied with a job or major (I/O psychology can help you determine what aspect is dissatisfying or what job/major would fit you better)
- Struggling with difficult coursework (I/O psychology provides training principles that can help motivate students and ensure that they retain what they learn)

HIGHLIGHTED STUDY FOR DISCUSSION

SIOP Member Survey

Although it is not a journal article, having students read a SIOP member survey (http://www.siop.org/surveys.aspx) can help them get a sense of what types of jobs exist for SIOP members and what the pay is for different types of jobs. This report is long, though most of the pages contain tables, so there isn't quite as much text for students to read as it first appears. Some key points of the 2012 survey results are as follows:

- Salaries appear to be getting higher over time (i.e., the median reported salary in 2012 was higher than it was in 2009 and 2006).
- Salaries tend to be higher in areas that have a high cost of living, such as Manhattan, San Francisco/San Jose, and Washington, DC.
- The median income of women was 12.1% lower than that of men; the report suggests that this may be partially due to the higher number of women earning MA degrees instead of PhDs, the fact that women work fewer hours, and the fact that women are less likely to own their own consulting business; however, this can be a good place to discuss whether the pay difference is fair.
- Respondents who were older and had earned their degree a long time ago tended to make more than young and new I/O psychologists. This finding may provide an interesting discussion point in terms of why this might be the case (e.g., a higher cumulative number of raises, more experience leading to higher pay).
- The majority of I/O psychologists work in consulting organizations or in colleges/universities. However, there are a variety of other organizations where I/O psychologists work (e.g., pharmaceutical companies, government entities, the military, nonprofits, IT companies).

■ The starting salary for someone with a PhD is about $15,000 more than for someone with an MA degree. You may want to discuss the pros and cons of getting a master's degree compared to a PhD (e.g., lower earnings, less time in school, fewer student loans, more difficulty moving up in a company).

■ The survey also revealed that 2.6% of all respondents had lost their job due to the recession, and that unemployment after job loss lasted an average of 4 months. In addition, 3.8% of respondents indicated that they had experienced a salary reduction in the aftermath of the recession, with the greatest number of salary reductions affecting those working in consulting firms, followed by universities and colleges. Finally, 5.3% of respondents indicated that they are working in jobs below their qualifications (a condition referred to as *underemployment*, which is discussed in Chapter 11). These findings could provide an opportunity to discuss the recession and job loss not only in abstract terms, but also in ways that directly affect the I/O practitioner and researcher.

WEB LEARNING

Title	Address
Society for Industrial and Organizational Psychology (SIOP)	http://www.siop.org
Academy of Management (AOM)	http://www.aomonline.org
Society for Human Resource Management (SHRM)	http://www.shrm.org
American Psychological Association (APA)	http://www.apa.org
Association for Psychological Science (APS)	http://www.psychologicalscience.org
International Association of Applied Psychology (IAAP)	http://www.iaapsy.org
Center for the History of Psychology	http://www.uakron.edu/chp

CHAPTER 2

Research Methods in I/O Psychology

LEARNING OBJECTIVES

This chapter should help students understand:

- The scientific method and its goals and assumptions
- The importance of theory to science and psychology
- Internal and external validity
- The complex interplay among experimental variables
- How research is conducted, with an emphasis on induction and deduction as well as the five steps involved in the process
- A variety of measurement issues such as reliability and validity
- Basic-level statistics ranging from descriptive statistics to correlation and regression

Chapter Summary

Research methods are important to I/O psychology—and all scientific endeavors, for that matter—because research conducted without care is unreliable and worthless. But when we are careful to base our theories on data and to use these data to test and revise the theories, the science of I/O psychology can make a meaningful contribution to the world of work. This science is more than just a matter of commonsense predictions and beliefs. Among its goals are to describe, explain, predict, and control human behavior at work. It is also important to realize that theories are the domain not just of basic science but also of applied scientific disciplines such as I/O psychology. In fact, it is only through careful theoretical development, testing, and revision that we can use our knowledge to describe, explain, predict, and control organizational behaviors and environments.

A major goal of most research in I/O psychology is to be able to draw causal inferences about the relationship between two or more variables. Thus, we must design our studies with an emphasis on internal validity, attempting to control for extraneous variables that could provide alternative explanations for our results. In addition to internal validity, we must concern ourselves with external validity, or the generalizability of our findings.

There are many ways in which I/O psychologists go about collecting data, but the survey is perhaps the one most frequently used. Surveys are very useful in gathering information about attitudes and beliefs. Technological advancements in the use of smartphones and other mobile devices have provided new alternative approaches to survey administration. We may also use observational approaches to measure and record frequency or incidents of particular behaviors or interactions. Archival research is a popular approach as well, given our access to the numerous large-scale data sets that have been collected by the government and private organizations. I/O psychologists often combine these and other data collection techniques in any given study to better examine their research questions.

Without reliable and valid measurement, the research conducted by I/O psychologists would have very little to offer. Researchers must work very hard to eliminate sources of measurement error and to ensure that their measures are tapping the constructs that they were intended to tap. There are a few different approaches to estimating reliability, and each is important for demonstrating the soundness of any particular measure. Validity is important as well, but to talk of validity in general is not very helpful, as the term can mean several different things. In I/O psychology, when we speak of the validity of a test or predictor, we are usually referring to the extent to which the test predicts job performance or some other criterion.

After we have collected our data, the next step is to describe and summarize those data using descriptive statistics such as measures of central tendency and dispersion. Because I/O psychologists are usually interested in the relationships among variables and the prediction of one set of variables from another set, correlation and regression are statistical techniques that are very useful to us. Ultimately, we complete our five-step research process with a written report that summarizes the research project.

In the remainder of this text, we will discuss various content areas of I/O psychology and the research that is conducted in those areas, along with their implications for organizational functioning.

TEACHING THE CHAPTER

Mastery of research methods and statistical concepts is a requirement for practicing I/O psychology. As such, it is important that the basic principles in this second chapter be presented clearly and effectively so that students have a solid foundation for understanding the material in the remainder of the textbook. Students are often uncomfortable and apprehensive about approaching statistics and research methods. Thus, clearly presenting this chapter's material and providing opportunities for students to engage in exercises that demonstrate the applicability of I/O research to real organizational issues is vital to ensuring that they will comprehend subsequent material in this book.

Instructors face at least four major challenges when teaching the material in this chapter. First, it may be difficult for students to comprehend that science is, according to Karl Popper, all about ruling out alternative explanations so that we can support a theory. Everyone is more comfortable when we can "prove" something, but, as you well know, in I/O psychology and in science, we cannot really prove anything. Thus, it may be worth pointing out to students that in many studies "significant" findings can explain as little as 10% of the variance in a dependent variable. So, even though 90% of variance remains unexplained, the results can be very important for theory building. As social scientists, we must continually refine and adapt our research questions to modern settings, a process that keeps us engaged in interesting and important research.

A second major issue for students in this chapter surrounds confusion about causal relationships and correlational relationships. When first introduced to research design and statistics, many students misinterpret large correlations between independent and dependent variables (IVs and DVs, respectively) as a causal relationship. Thus, it is important to clearly explain the importance of research design, the roles of IVs and DVs, and the concept of experimental control. Some of the chapter exercises have been designed to address this very issue by clarifying these concepts. You may want to select research studies using organizational samples that have been published in reputable journals (e.g., *Journal of Applied Psychology*, *Academy of Management Journal*) to illustrate and clarify the topics of research control and causal inference.

Third, understanding the important concepts of reliability and validity of measures in I/O psychology is critical because they reemerge in subsequent chapters dealing with selection, predictors, and performance appraisal. The earlier in the course that students comprehend the importance of reliable and valid construct measurement, the greater the benefit and understanding they will have when these topics are discussed later in the semester. Before drilling down into statistical issues, consider helping students focus on the conceptual meaning and significance of *reliability* (measurement consistency) and *validity* (measurement precision).

Finally, though some of the statistical concepts presented in the chapter should be familiar to students, they will undoubtedly benefit from a comprehensive review of the concepts of central tendency, the properties of dispersion, and a reminder of what the correlation coefficient means to research.

The following suggested exercises have been designed to help you encourage students to apply their thinking and discuss research methods. Any review of research methods should contain considerable discussion about research design and relevant considerations when setting up a research study. The first exercise involves designing a training study to improve the test scores of students in a class. Aside from providing a wonderful opportunity to discuss and clarify IVs and DVs and to consider the consequences of different research designs, this exercise can also supplement student learning by promoting an active discussion about the ethics of using a control group in the study.

We also encourage you to assign students to use a library database to identify a research study from an I/O journal and present its key points to the class. This exercise can help students identify the important points to take away from research studies and provide valuable practice in reading I/O literature. Alternatively, you can assign students to locate an article on a given course topic, ensuring that all course topics are covered. Then, on the day that topic is discussed, have one or more students present an article on it. This can help break up the monotony of lectures, help students sharpen their presentation skills, and give the class additional exposure to research on I/O topics.

SUGGESTED EXERCISES AND ASSIGNMENTS

Design an Experiment: Improving Test Performance

Purpose The objective of this exercise is to provide students with an opportunity to apply research method concepts from the textbook and lecture by creating their own research study. Students should find this exercise interesting because they are often concerned with their test scores and how they can improve them.

Instructions

- Divide the class into groups of four to six and ask them to develop a study designed to improve the test scores of students in the class.
- The intervention (training) can focus on improving study habits, increasing class attendance, or anything else that students can think of. Groups should identify:
  - The intervention (training) they will use to improve course grades
  - The hypothesis of the experiment
  - The independent variable
  - The dependent variable
  - The research design
  - Any potential extraneous variables

Discussion Questions

- What steps could be taken to control for extraneous variables?
- What other related dependent variables might we want to examine?
- What steps could be taken to ensure that this experiment is conducted in an ethical manner?

Article Retrieval

Purpose The objective of this exercise is to give students an opportunity to locate and read published research articles in the I/O literature and to increase their comfort level in reading scholarly work.

Instructions

- Students will need to use the library database to locate an article in an I/O journal on a topic that you designate or one that is of interest to them.
- At the start of the semester, you might want to consider assigning individual students (or groups of four to six) an article that is relevant to each course topic. Then have each student (or group) present the article on the day you teach the given topic.
- Students should identify and report the following information from the article(s):
  - Author, title, and publication date
  - Purpose of study
  - Hypotheses
  - Type of research method used
  - Statistics used
  - Sample population
  - Independent and dependent variables
  - Summary of research findings
- Suggested journals:
  - *Journal of Applied Psychology*
  - *Personnel Psychology*
  - *Academy of Management Journal*
  - *Journal of Management*
  - *Organizational Behavior and Human Decision Processes*
  - *Leadership Quarterly*

Discussion Questions

- Why is this research important to the practice and science of I/O psychology?
- What, if anything, could the researcher(s) have done to improve the study?

Becoming an Observer

Purpose The objective of this exercise is to give students the opportunity to practice and exercise observational skills and to report observations.

Instructions

- Ask students to observe and document the events that occur during a situation typical of their daily life.
  - *Suggested situations suitable for observation*: standing at a bus stop, sitting in the library, eating dinner, going to the gym
- Work together in class to identify one situation that all students will observe before a designated class period. Then identify all of the important variables that you want them to collect data on (e.g., numbers of people, topics of conversations).
- Once students have made their observations and documented the behaviors, have them present their findings to the class (or in small groups).

Discussion Questions

- What are the main similarities in your observations? The main differences?
- Why do you think there were differences in your observations?
- What, if any, difficulties did you encounter when observing the situation?
- What could be done to make your reports more consistent?

Debate

Purpose The objective of the exercise is to give students the opportunity to debate issues relating to survey research in organizations.

Instructions

- Inform students that they are a team of I/O psychologists interested in surveying employees to learn about the effects of Internet use on employee work performance.
- Divide the class into several small groups of four to six students.
- Assign groups to the following positions:
  - In favor of smartphone surveys
  - In favor of mail surveys
  - In favor of interviews
- Have the groups outline the benefits of their assigned survey type. They should also be prepared to defend the drawbacks of their survey type.

Discussion Questions

- How does the cost of administering the survey affect the type of survey you would give?
- What (if any) ethical concerns might there be in this type of research?

Archival Research

Purpose The objective of this exercise is to give students an opportunity to carry out archival research that relates directly to I/O concepts.

Instructions

- Ask student to consider what skills, traits, or abilities might be required in the workplace. Divide students into groups and ask them to create a short list (e.g., five to seven items) of qualifications they believe organizations will expect of their applicants.
- Ask groups to examine a source where job opportunities are listed (e.g., an online resource such as Craigslist.com or Monster.com or a newspaper). Ask them to randomly choose 20 ads and put a checkmark next to each qualification when they see it mentioned in these ads.
- When students have had enough time to complete the task, ask them to come back together into a larger group.

Discussion Questions

- What characteristics seemed to be most important to organizations? Least important?
- Is this a representative sample of organizations? Why or why not?
- Do you think you will have these commonly requested skills/abilities when you complete college? If not, what can you do to acquire them?

Observational Research

Purpose In this exercise, students will both learn a method of research and become aware of some of the difficulties with this approach.

- Obtain a short television episode or short movie clip. Prior to class, view the clip and identify a construct that is potentially tricky to operationally define but possible to observe. For example, you can ask students to identify an act of aggression in a children's cartoon. Or you can ask students to identify acts of sexism, leadership, harassment, or something similar in an episode of a workplace sitcom (such as *The Office, Parks and Recreation,* or *Better Off Ted*) or reality shows (such as *Undercover Boss*).
- Ask students to observe the clip you have selected and briefly jot down a note about each instance of the target construct.
- Once the clip has ended, ask students to turn to a nearby student to compare notes.
- Students are likely to note that there are some differences in what they have identified. For example, if one character says something mean to another character, some students may not have identified that behavior as aggressive. Or if a female character tells a male character to "be a man" about something, some students may not identify this as sexist behavior.

Discussion Questions

- How did you operationally define your variable?
- Did you find it difficult to determine whether any behaviors you saw should be included as examples of the target construct? Why was this difficult?
- What does this exercise demonstrate about operational definitions and constructs?

EVALUATING "TAKING IT TO THE FIELD"

This chapter's "Taking It to the Field" exercise dealt with an e-mail from Kendall Phillips, the HR manager of the law firm MacLaughlin & MacDougal. She designed a new selection measure for her firm and needs some feedback from someone who knows more about reliability and validity. There are many possible responses to the scenario, but the points below are suggestions for what poor, good, and excellent responses should look like.

Reliability

Poor responses...	■ Are based primarily on the student's gut feelings or impressions and demonstrate little critical thinking (e.g., "I think that you did a great job making your test!").
	■ Fail to indicate which types of reliability are covered or use terms inappropriately (e.g., referring to test–retest reliability as internal consistency).
	■ Suggest that Kendall must establish interrater reliability. In this case, there is no real need for interrater reliability because there are no observations/ratings taking place.
Good responses...	■ Clearly indicate that the test has .89 test–retest reliability and indicate that this is above the usual .70 minimum.
	■ Indicate that Kendall does not have any measure of internal consistency and that she should consider assessing this.
Excellent responses...	■ Clearly indicate that the test has .89 test–retest reliability and that this is above the usual .70 minimum.
	■ Indicate that Kendall does not have any measure of internal consistency and suggest that she use her existing data to calculate this (using split halves, Cronbach's alpha, or the Kuder-Richardson 20).
	■ Suggest that Kendall also consider creating an alternate version of the test (so that if there is a mistake, someone can retake it) and encourage her to establish parallel forms reliability.
	■ Do NOT suggest establishing interrater reliability (as there are no raters in this scenario).

Validity

Poor responses...	■ Are based primarily on the student's gut feelings or impressions and demonstrate little critical thinking (e.g., "I think that you did a great job making your test!").
	■ Fail to indicate which types of validity are covered or use terms inappropriately (e.g., referring to content validity as construct validity).
	■ Fail to clearly demonstrate knowledge of which statistical evidence relates to each type of validity if specific types of validity are mentioned (e.g., telling Kendall that she has adequate divergent validity without indicating which statistic refers to that validity).

Good responses...	■ Discuss whether Kendall has established content validity. There can be some debate here—students may argue that because she has consulted with experts and looked at similar tests, she has done what she can to establish this. Alternatively, students might ask to see the test items or suggest that Kendall have one of her experts look over the test to ensure that it covers all aspects of neuroticism. ■ Indicate that Kendall has partially satisfied the requirements for criterion-related validity. The correlation between the NAF and performance ($r = .30$) represents concurrent validity. ■ Indicate that Kendall has provided both convergent validity ($r = .75$) and divergent validity ($r = .34$). Because the convergent validity is relatively high and the divergent validity is relatively low, she has demonstrated that her instrument appears to measure neuroticism, not some other construct. Note that students are often confused about divergent validity, so it will be helpful to provide feedback if they make a mistake on this point.
Excellent responses...	■ Discuss whether Kendall has established content validity. There can be some debate here—students may argue that because she has consulted with experts and looked at similar tests, she has done what she can to establish this. Alternatively, students might ask to see the test items or suggest that Kendall have one of her experts look over the test to ensure that it covers all aspects of neuroticism. ■ Indicate that Kendall has partially satisfied the requirements for criterion-related validity. The correlation between the NAF and performance ($r = .30$) represents concurrent validity. Excellent responses will also note that she does not have predictive validity and may suggest that she begin administering this measure to job applicants to see if it also predicts performance. ■ Indicate that Kendall has provided both convergent validity ($r = .75$) and divergent validity ($r = .34$). Because the convergent validity is relatively high and the divergent validity is relatively low, she has demonstrated that her instrument appears to measure neuroticism, not some other construct. ■ Mention construct validity. Students should indicate that the above components (content validity, criterion-related validity, convergent and divergent validity) indicate whether the measure has construct validity. Because construct validity is somewhat subjective, students can either agree or disagree that the measure is valid, as long as they indicate why they believe so.

EVALUATING "APPLICATION QUESTIONS"

1. Imagine that a fellow student says to you, "I don't need a study to tell me that lecturing is a bad way to teach students. I know from my own experience that it never works!" How would you convince this student of the value of research? What might be an example of a study you could conduct to see if this student's belief is accurate?

   Evaluation Guide: Students may have a variety of responses to this statement. Some examples might be:
   - Students may note that this student's experience may not be accurate or relevant to other students (e.g., this student may not take classes where lecture is effective; this student may have had unskilled lecturers; some people may learn better from lectures than from other methods).
   - Students may also note that this student's statement is not precise. What does the student mean by "a bad way to teach"? Does this mean that lectures are boring? That most students don't remember what they hear?
   - Students may also note that this student is not precise about what he or she means by "lecture"—some lectures incorporate interesting examples and discussions, while others simply restate content from the book.
   - Finally, students may point out that "never" is an overgeneralization. Lectures may work sometimes, in some situations, for some people, and for some topics.
   - Students will likely have a number of ideas for research, but probably the best option is to conduct an experiment in which students are taught about a topic in a lecture versus another method (e.g., group activity, video, or discussion). Depending on how well the students perform on a test assessing whether they have learned and understood the content, we can determine whether one method of teaching is more effective than another.

2. Think about a behavior you have observed among fellow students. What do you think causes that behavior, and what might be a theory you can develop to explain why that behavior occurs?

   Evaluation Guide: Students may come up with a variety of interesting observations and theories. It may help to address the following topics:
   - Does the theory describe the behavior? If not, how can students be more specific in describing a behavior? For example, if a student observes that men and women listen to music "differently," ask for a more detailed explanation of what is meant by "differently" (e.g., different types of music, different volume, use of earphones versus speakers).
   - Does the theory explain why a behavior occurs? If a student states that women are more likely to wear earbuds to listen to music, while men are more likely to use headphones, ask why might this be. What is it that might make women prefer earbuds (e.g., better fit for smaller ears, doesn't interfere with hairstyles)?

- Does the theory help predict what someone might do? For example, if I own an electronics store, how might this theory help me decide what types of inventory to carry if a lot of women shop there?

3. A researcher has been asked to find a way to help construction workers put on their helmets. Describe a survey study she could conduct. What information would she get from that study? Describe an experimental study she could conduct. What information would she get from that study?

Evaluation Guide: Students may come up with a variety of ideas. However, strong responses will address the following issues:

- For the survey study, students should identify questions they might ask the construction workers (e.g., "What are some reasons why you do not wear your hard hat? How often do you forget to wear your hard hat? Is your hard hat comfortable?"). However, students should also recognize that because construction workers are reporting on their own behavior, their judgments may or may not be accurate.
- For the experiment, students should suggest changing something to see if that encourages the construction workers to wear their hard hats (e.g., putting up signs, making hats more comfortable). The researcher then might measure whether construction workers wear their hard hats more after she has implemented the change (or, alternatively, students might suggest she change something at one site and not at another, so she can compare the two groups of construction workers). Students should recognize that this would allow the researcher to assume causality (e.g., putting up signs causes construction workers to remember to put on their hard hats).

4. Reliability and validity are two separate characteristics of a measurement, but they are related. The chapter notes that you must have reliability (consistency) before you can have validity (accuracy). Provide an example of a measure that is consistent but inaccurate.

Evaluation Guide: Students often find this topic to be quite difficult, so this allows you to identify confusion or misunderstandings. Common examples might include the following:

- A clock might be set to the wrong time. This clock is consistent (it can still tell you how long a minute is), but it is inaccurate (it is telling you the wrong time).
- A scale might be calibrated incorrectly. This scale is consistent (you can step on it every day, and every day the scale will read 180 pounds), but it is inaccurate (if you actually only weigh 120 pounds).
- Many women's and men's magazines have quizzes that purport to measure personality by asking questions about how you decorate or what foods you like. These measures might be consistent (you can get the same score each time you take it), but they are probably not accurate (liking cheesecake probably does not say anything much about your personality).

5. Correlation coefficients can help us understand how two variables are related. What are two variables that might have a strong, positive correlation? A strong negative correlation? A correlation of 0?

Evaluation Guide: Students typically can easily come up with a few examples of each. Some topics that emerge might be:

- If one student expects a positive relationship between two variables, and other students disagree, you can discuss the importance of theory. For example, one student might believe that if a boss is rude, there will be less cooperation among team members (because team members take out their frustrations on one another); another student might believe that the opposite result is likely (because the coworkers see the boss as a common enemy, they will be more supportive of and cooperative with one another). This might lead to a discussion about how many theories can contradict one another and how empirical investigation can determine which one is likely to apply in a certain situation.

- Students may struggle to think of examples in which there is no relationship between variables. Sometimes choosing silly variables can help (e.g., there is no correlation between how many hours you spend in a car per day and how many pairs of scissors you own). This can also help demonstrate that variables that aren't correlated typically are not very interesting to most scientists!

HIGHLIGHTED STUDY FOR DISCUSSION

Fine, M. A., & Kurdik, L. A. (1993). Reflections on determining authorship credit and authorship order on faculty-student collaborations. *American Psychologist, 48,* 1141–1147.

This article discusses a number of the concerns that faculty and students might consider when publishing a paper together. The article provides some nice insights into some of the issues at hand in research that may not always be considered by researchers at the outset. It provides several scenarios, as well as the authors' opinions on how credit should be awarded. The scenarios are as follows:

- *Case 1:* A student develops an idea with his practicum supervisor. The student, his practicum supervisor, and the dissertation committee chair agree to publish the paper, with the student as first author, the practicum supervisor as second author, and the committee chair as third author. However, after several drafts, the student loses interest, and ultimately the committee chair takes over the paper and conducts extensive reanalysis of the data.

- *Case 2:* An undergraduate student and her advisor work together on an undergraduate honors thesis. The student comes up with the initial idea, collects the data, and writes drafts of the paper. The advisor clarifies the research methodology, conducts the statistical analysis, and edits the final paper. One-third of the final paper is made up of portions of the student's thesis.

- *Case 3:* A psychologist and a psychiatrist design a study and invited a master's student to help with the paper. The student finds several additional articles, collects and analyzes the data, and writes a thesis under the supervision of the psychologist. After the defense, the paper requires some reanalysis and writing to be ready for publication. The student is not asked to help with this part.
- *Case 4:* An undergraduate and faculty member work together on an undergraduate thesis project. The student and faculty member design a measure together. The student collects the data and writes the paper. The faculty member helps with the statistical analyses. The paper needs revisions to become an empirical article, which is done by the professor. In the revision, they need to use aspects of the study not included in the original thesis, and it will require a major rewrite.
- The authors present their perspective on considerations for deciding authorship and suggest the following for each case:
  - In Case 1, the student deserves authorship because of his contribution to the paper, but perhaps not first authorship if he drops out of the project. The supervisor's contribution should also be carefully considered when deciding authorship.
  - In Case 2, the student should be given first authorship if she continues to work on the paper to make it into a publishable article. If not, she should still receive second authorship, with a note in the article that it was based on her honor's thesis.
  - In Case 3, the student should be given third authorship, as he contributed what was expected and to the utmost extent of his professional capabilities.
  - In Case 4, the student should be offered an opportunity to participate in the rewrite; if she accepts, she should be given first authorship.
- Additional discussion points with your class might center around what constitutes "work" and reward in these contexts. It might also be helpful to ask students not to read the authors' recommendations and instead to consider what they think would be fair in each scenario. Students can then discuss how they define "fair" and consider the implications of their definitions on both the student and the faculty member or supervisor.

WEB LEARNING

Title	Address
APA Ethical Principles of Psychologists and Code of Conduct	http://www.apa.org/ethics/code/index.aspx
Academy of Management Research Methods Division	http://rmdiv.org/
American Statistical Association (ASA)	http://www.amstat.org
StatSoft: *Electronic Statistics Textbook*	http://www.statsoft.com/Textbook
Statistics for Psychologists	http://www.psychwww.com/resource/bytopic/stats.html
Hyperstat Online: An introductory statistics book	http://www.davidmlane.com/hyperstat/intro.html
Web Center for Social Research Methods	http://www.socialresearchmethods.net
Organizational Research Methods (journal, requires subscription)	http://orm.sagepub.com
Creative Research Systems: A survey design tutorial	http://www.surveysystem.com/sdesign.htm
Rice Virtual Lab in Statistics: Simulations and demonstrations of statistics	http://onlinestatbook.com/stat_sim/
Interpreting Correlations: An interactive visualization	http://rpsychologist.com/d3/correlation/
JASP: A free statistical analysis program	https://jasp-stats.org/

Job Analysis

This chapter should help students understand:

- How important job analysis is to HR functioning
- The common terminology used in the area of job analysis
- How to differentiate between task-oriented and worker-oriented job analysis techniques
- How to conduct a job analysis using the Task Inventory Approach, Functional Job Analysis, Job Element Method, Position Analysis Questionnaire, and Common-Metric Questionnaire
- What's included in the *Dictionary of Occupational Titles* and how it has been improved through the development of the Occupational Information Network (O*NET)
- What a job description is and how it is used in human resource practices
- What job specifications are and how they are used in human resource practices
- The variety of human resource functions for which job analysis is of great importance
- The newly developing role of technology in the analysis of jobs
- The role of job evaluation in setting compensation levels
- The doctrine of comparable worth and the wage gap

Chapter Summary

Although job analysis tends to receive little empirical attention, it is among the most important areas of I/O psychology, providing the foundation on which all other HR processes are built. This chapter was largely structured around Figure 3.1, which shows the interrelationships among job analysis, job descriptions, job specifications, job evaluation, and the HR functions that are built on these processes. It should be clear by now that without a carefully designed and executed job analysis, HR practitioners and I/O psychologists would have very little to go on in making HR decisions.

Both task–oriented and worker-oriented approaches to job analysis were presented in this chapter, along with a discussion of different methods within each category.

Also discussed were the advantages and disadvantages of each approach, the choice of which should depend on the job analyst's purpose. Some developments in the area of job analysis were considered as well. First, although the DOT has been of great importance to the I/O field for many years, the Department of Labor's current undertaking, the O★NET should provide more updated, useful, and accessible data on occupations and jobs. Second, the CMQ was presented as one of the newer job analysis instruments with great potential to serve the purposes of worker-oriented job analysis methods while avoiding criticisms regarding reading level and work behaviors that are too general.

Job descriptions and job specifications are derived either directly or indirectly from the job analysis and are directly or indirectly connected to a myriad of HR functions. This chapter provided a brief discussion of the links between job analysis and these HR functions; the remainder of the second part of the text will cover these HR functions at length. Finally, we considered the role of job analysis in job evaluation. The Equal Pay Act of 1963 mandates that individuals who do equal work should receive equal pay, but it does not speak to wage gaps between "male-typed" and "female-typed" jobs. The emergence of the doctrine of comparable worth suggests that organizations and society need to do a better job in setting compensation for jobs while taking gender-based job classes into account.

TEACHING THE CHAPTER

Job analysis is the foundation for the "I" (industrial) component of I/O psychology. I/O psychologists rely on job analysis data to design selection systems, performance appraisal instruments, and training programs and to select criteria for measuring work performance. For this reason, ensuring that students understand the material in this chapter is paramount to their comprehension of subsequent topics discussed in this book. From their reading, your lecture, and the class exercises, students should gain an understanding of the components of job analysis as well as the types of information collected and recorded during the process.

In this chapter, the technical issues, approaches, and methodologies involved in job analysis are discussed thoroughly. As an instructor, you can choose to emphasize either task-oriented or worker-oriented methodologies (or both) in class assignments. But regardless of the methodology you emphasize in class activities or assignments, this chapter provides the foundation for explaining the use of job analysis for I/O psychologists, HR functioning, and organizational effectiveness.

To supplement chapter reading and lectures, students should be engaged in activities and assignments that focus on applying their knowledge to an actual job analysis project. The following section provides several activities designed to enhance textbook material. The activities will also help to develop students' practical knowledge and experience in the classroom and extend it toward a larger assignment that can be used throughout the semester as a resource for class exercises.

The first exercise is designed to get students thinking about the types of KSAOs and the level of investigatory work necessary for conducting a job analysis. By working to identify the knowledge, skills, abilities, and other requirements of psychology professors and students, your class will learn about the details that an effective job analysis should capture. This exercise also may stimulate a lively class discussion about academic responsibility. The remaining exercises/assignments can be conducted in class or given as assignments to provide your students with applied job analysis experience. Because job analysis is the basis for so many other I/O activities, the job analysis assignment should be framed with a semester-length scope, requiring students to reference the data they collect in the job analysis for forthcoming projects (e.g., designing a job advertisement and a performance appraisal instrument).

SUGGESTED EXERCISES AND ASSIGNMENTS

KSAOs for College Students and Psychology Professors

Purpose Through this exercise, students will gain insight into the jobs of students and professors in the academic environment as well as what each party must bring to the class in order to create an effective educational experience.

Instructions
- *Prior to class:* Visit the O★NET website (http://online.onetcenter.org) and look up the listing for a psychology professor (SOC code: 25-1066.00: "Psychology Teachers, Postsecondary"). Using the "Occupation Quick Search" field, enter "Psychology Professor" to quickly go to the listing. If your classroom has multimedia (i.e., Internet access), you could bookmark the page so you can show it to students after they have completed this activity. Otherwise, you could print the classification's "Summary" page to show the class.
- Break the class into small groups and ask them to brainstorm about the KSAOs that are required to be a college student and a psychology professor. Also, time permitting, they should brainstorm task requirements for each job.
- Ask groups to share the KSAOs and tasks that they identified for each role. Create a class list that contains the unique KSAOs and tasks for each role. Each group will likely have unique contributions to these lists.
- After students have generated their lists and shared them with the class, share the O★NET list of the KSAOs and task requirements of a psychology professor.

Discussion Questions
- To what extent have we adequately described our roles as professor and students?
- Does the O★NET adequately describe the professor's role? Are there any areas of a professor's job that this description has omitted?

- Since the O★NET already contains so much information, why do I/O psychologists conduct job analyses instead of simply referring to this comprehensive database?
- How could an I/O practitioner use the information from the O★NET?

Developing Questions to Gather Job Analysis Information

Purpose In this exercise, students will consider the questions they would use when interviewing job incumbents to collect job analysis information and to generate a set of questions they can use in their own job analysis assignments.

Instructions

- *Prior to class:* Create a handout that outlines the critical information that must be collected in a job analysis:
  - A definition of knowledge, skills, abilities, and other characteristics along with an explanation of how each K, S, A, or O is different from the others
  - A definition of task requirements and work environment characteristics
  - A way to differentiate between essential and nonessential tasks
- Consider dividing the class into small groups. Or simply conduct this as an open class discussion if your class is not too large.
- Provide the handout outlining the necessary information to students.
- To ensure that students understand the differences between knowledge (K), skills (S), and abilities (A), you might provide examples and ask the class to identify each as a K, S, or A. For example, is being fluent in a second language a knowledge, skill, or ability? One must have knowledge of the language but must also be able to speak it well. Are skills manual-type activities (like typing or digging), or can speaking another language also be a skill? Stimulate class thinking about the challenges in classifying behaviors as K, S, or A.
- Have students brainstorm a set of approximately 10 questions, including any necessary follow-up questions they would use when interviewing a job incumbent.
- Have individuals/groups turn to other individuals/groups and share their list of questions to receive feedback on its comprehensiveness and effectiveness.
- As an outcome of this exercise, a "job analysis questions" handout can be generated for students' use in conducting their own job incumbent interviews.

Discussion Questions

- Did you receive any surprising feedback from other groups? What are some examples?
- What were some aspects of the job that you overlooked?
- What did you find more challenging than you expected during this exercise?
- How do you think answers to these questions might differ if you interview a supervisor instead of a job incumbent?

Job Analysis

Purpose Students will conduct an abbreviated version of a job analysis in a "safe" environment (i.e., they interview a friend or family member and write up the results for class instead of an organization).

Instructions

- Ask students to conduct a job analysis by interviewing a friend or family member who is currently employed. Information should include (but not be limited to) the following:
  - An overall description of the job
  - An explanation of how the job is classified in the O★NET (including the occupational code and task requirements)
  - A description of the knowledge, skills, abilities, and other characteristics that are essential to job performance (based on student findings, not the O★NET)
  - A description of the work environment, including a description of the physical work environment, supervisory controls, physical demands, typical amount of interpersonal contact, amount of expected teamwork, job complexity, and amount of direction (supervision) typically required to get the job done (again, based on student findings, not the O★NET)
  - A brief summary of the organization's culture and competitive environment
- Have students write their job analysis, including the information presented above. They should also outline any challenges they faced in interviewing the incumbent and writing the job analysis. Write-ups can be anywhere from two to five pages in length.
- If feasible, have students present their job analysis findings to the class.

Discussion Questions

- Were there any aspects of the job that you were surprised by? What are some examples?
- What challenges did you face while you were working on this assignment?
- How do you think your results might have differed if you interviewed a different person in this position at this organization?
- What would differ if you interviewed someone in the same position in a different organization?
- Why is accuracy so important in job analysis? What are some barriers to obtaining accurate responses from your interviewee?

Design a Job Advertisement

Purpose Students will apply information from their job analysis to a real-world application.

Instructions

- *Prior to class:* Prepare a sample job analysis before class to present to students (this can be the psychology professor O★NET description). Or have students bring a copy of their job analysis to class.
- Divide students into groups of three or four.
- Have students select one group member's job analysis to use in writing a job advertisement. Once they have selected the job, they should generate a fictional organization where the job is located.
- Have students create a brief advertisement for the job, including the following:
  - An accurate description of the task requirements for the job
  - A brief list of applicant requirements
  - Something that "sells" the organization to potential applicants
- Have students share their job advertisements with the class. You might consider having students vote on the most desirable job based on the advertisements.

Discussion Questions

- Was there any information that you would have liked to have, but was not available, when you created the job description?
- Would you apply for a job like the one you are advertising based on the advertisement you created? Why or why not?
- What job advertisements have you seen that attracted you to apply for a job?

Conduct a Job Evaluation

Purpose Students will consider what types of factors lead to different pay in organizations.

Instructions

- *Prior to class:* Consider an organization with which students are likely to have had experience. For example, they can consider jobs on a college campus or in an organization for which they have worked or been a customer (e.g., a grocery store, restaurant, or a retail outlet).
- Divide students into groups of three or four. Ask them to think of three jobs in the target organization and consider the following:
  - How much *effort* is involved in each job?
  - How much *skill* is required by the job?
  - How much *responsibility* is required by the job?
  - What are the *working conditions* of the job?
- Ask students to use their answers to these questions to estimate the annual salary for each position (these will likely be rather high compared to what would be realistic).
- Have students share the jobs they considered and their estimated salaries.

Discussion Questions

- How important did you consider each component when deciding how much to pay each person? Did you tend to weight one aspect more heavily than others when you were estimating salaries?
- What information would you have liked to have? How might you go about getting that information?

EVALUATING "TAKING IT TO THE FIELD"

The Chapter 3 activity involves having students interview college employees to learn more about what characteristics are required to be effective at a certain job. We use this approach so that students can also learn more about their college/university. However, if you have concerns about receiving a number of varied responses, you can also ask the students to do a job analysis for an employee they all have access to (e.g., a college professor) or you can ask them to create a job description for a position they are likely to be familiar with (e.g., a fast-food cook, a server in a restaurant).

Below is a general rubric for what poor, good, and excellent responses look like.

Poor responses…	■ Contain spelling and grammatical errors. ■ Are copied directly from O*NET. ■ Use inconsistent verb tenses (e.g., *listens, observed*). ■ Are too vague to provide useful information about the job (e.g., "Knows how to clean"). ■ Provide the response in an essay-style format. ■ Focus on job tasks (e.g., "Cleans tables properly"). ■ Are too short (e.g., less than a half a page) or too long (over two pages).
Good responses…	■ Use proper spelling and grammar. ■ Use a consistent verb tense (e.g., *listens, observes*). ■ Provide adequate detail for an applicant to understand a position (e.g., "Knows how to properly disinfect a food preparation area"). ■ Effectively use bullet points. ■ Are an appropriate length (one to two pages).
Excellent responses…	■ Use flawless spelling and grammar. ■ Use a consistent verb tense. ■ Provide adequate detail for an applicant to understand a position (e.g., "Knows how to properly disinfect a food preparation area"). ■ Effectively use bullet points. ■ Are an appropriate length (one to two pages). ■ Note details about workers that other students may take for granted (e.g., whether speaking English is necessary, whether good vision is required for the job).

EVALUATING "APPLICATION QUESTIONS"

1. Find an online job posting. According to this posting, what are some KSAOs required for that position? Are there any KSAOs you believe might be expected but are omitted from this ad? What might be the consequences of this omission?

   Evaluation Guide: Responses from students may vary a great deal in this activity. So you might ask to see the ad as well as students' responses so you can better evaluate how well they have identified key points. Here are some points you might consider making:
   - There may be some expectations that are assumed on the part of the HR department and thus are not mentioned in the job ad. For example, sometimes job ads omit information about being able to work with others, having writing skills, or being able to work with ambiguous or poorly defined problems.
   - There are some KSAOs that are likely to be common across ads. This might be a good opportunity to connect students' college experiences with these ads. For example, if many ads stipulate the importance of having good interpersonal skills, you might discuss with students how they can work on building these skills during their time in college.

2. Consider a position you currently hold or that you have held in the past. What pieces of information about your job did you know well that you could share with a job analyst? What pieces of information did you not know? Who in the organization would have been better equipped to provide this information to a job analyst?

   Evaluation Guide: Responses from students will vary a great deal, and students may need some prompting to come up with ideas for what information they might have missed in their role. Below are some points you may consider making:
   - Students are likely to know a great deal about behaviors and skills that are necessary, especially those that might not be apparent to a casual observer (e.g., extra tasks they do in the back room, or tasks that are important, but rarely done). Students often don't know what the gaps are in their knowledge, so getting answers to this question may take some prompting.
   - Students are less likely to know information about how their position compared to other jobs within and outside of the company. Furthermore, they may not understand how their job fits into the organization on a larger scale. Students also may not have much information about what they didn't know about their job (e.g., tasks they didn't realize they were responsible for). Supervisors or other leaders, and job analysts may have a better sense of these issues. Advantages of using supervisors include that they may have a good sense of which KSAOs are most important to the mission of the organization, and they may be more objective than job incumbents about which KSAOs are

important. Some disadvantages include that they may not be aware of some of the day-to-day minutiae, and they may not know about KSAOs that are rare or not easily observable.

3. Imagine that your college or university is considering using a competency model to ensure that students who graduate have competencies that are necessary in the workplace. What might be some competencies that all students should master by the time they graduate?

   Evaluation Guide: Responses to this item may vary, but students should be able to identify competencies that are fairly broad in nature. Example responses may include the following:

   - With respect to any class in any college/university, competencies might include effective communication, effective writing, effective study skills, leadership skills, and ability to engage in teamwork. Encourage students to use broader competencies (e.g., effective communication) rather than specific tasks or characteristics (e.g., being proactive in asking an instructor for help).
   - With respect to competencies that might be unique to the student's institution, there may be unique skills or beliefs that are important for student success or self-esteem. For example, in religious institutions, demonstrating strong faith may be part of the student experience. In a school where volunteerism is a focus, interests and skills in this area may be relevant.
   - It is helpful to draw students' attention to the difference between competencies (which can be quite general) and a more task-oriented job analysis approach (which is quite specific).

4. Imagine you have a client who is hesitant to commit to a job analysis. She states that the investment of time and money into developing a job analysis for every position isn't worth it, especially because she thinks that many jobs in the organization will change a lot within the next five years. What might you say to this client?

   Evaluation Guide: Students may have a broad array of responses for this question. If they need prompting, you could encourage them to think about what jobs might be more important in the future work environment or how the changing nature of work and technology might affect the skills that are necessary. Here are some additional points to consider:

   - Students should consider the value of competency modeling or strategic job modeling to help establish KSAOs that can adapt to the changes this client thinks she will be making. For example, the client might want to think about what types of skills someone can use to help adapt to changes in the job— good critical thinking skills, an interest in learning new technologies, or good communication skills can all be beneficial for selecting an adaptable employee.
   - Students could also suggest to the client that she start with job analyses on positions that she doesn't expect to change much. For example, an HR position will likely not change much, while an assembly line position might change a lot if new technology is going to be installed soon.

HIGHLIGHTED STUDY FOR DISCUSSION

Landrum, R. E., Hettich, P. I., & Wilner, A. (2010). Alumni perceptions of workforce readiness. *Teaching of Psychology, 37,* 97–106.

Although not strictly about job analysis, this article provides an interesting example of a mismatch between individuals' skills and the jobs they hold. The article may also provide students some insight into how college can prepare them for the workforce and why instructors may make decisions about including particular projects or policies in the classroom. Key points in the article include the following:

- Several national surveys indicate that current employers are generally unsatisfied with the level of preparedness among recent college graduates.
- Three hundred and six Boise State University psychology alumni were mailed a survey regarding which skills they believed they gained in college and which they gained in the workplace. Seventy-eight of these were returned with usable data.
- The top 10 skills in terms of importance were the following:
  1. Possessing self-discipline (punctuality and responsibility)
  2. Acting responsibly
  3. Working with others
  4. Meeting the needs of others
  5. Setting priorities and managing time effectively
  6. Identifying and solving problems
  7. Making appropriate decisions
  8. Working without supervision
  9. Working independently
  10. Managing several tasks at once
- The authors also noted personality characteristics of alumni that changed a great deal after graduation. These included being more confident, independent, mature, and assertive as well as being less shy, resentful, and defensive.
- The authors also collected open-ended comments from alumni. Many of the comments related to how professors should use classroom assignments to help build needed skills. For example, respondents suggested that professors should be more stringent with deadlines and assignment completion because these qualities are expected in a work environment. Similarly, respondents noted the importance of group work in developing skills for working with other people.

WEB LEARNING

Title	Address
O*NET online	http://online.onetcenter.org
Dictionary of Occupational Titles, 4th edition	http://www.oalj.dol.gov/libdot.htm
HR-Guide.com	http://www.hr-guide.com
U.S. Department of Labor website	http://www.dol.gov
Job evaluation website (from HR-Guide.com)	http://www.hr-guide.com/jobevaluation.htm
Job classification website (from HR-Guide.com)	http://www.job-analysis.net/G010.htm
Equal Pay Act of 1963	http://www.eeoc.gov/policy/epa.html

Criterion Measurement

This chapter should help students understand:

- What the criterion problem is
- How criteria are defined in I/O psychology
- What the criteria for the criteria are
- The difference between the ultimate criterion and the actual criterion
- How to differentiate between criterion contamination and criterion deficiency
- The important issues that revolve around multiple criteria
- Different ways to weight criteria to arrive at a composite criterion
- What dynamic criteria are and how they can affect HR functioning
- The differences between objective and subjective criteria
- The potential role of contextual performance (including counterproductive behavior) in criterion development
- The complex relationships between task behavior, contextual behavior, and counterproductive work behavior

Chapter Summary

Traditionally, I/O psychologists have emphasized predictors at the expense of criteria. But this is less the case now that more and more scientists and practitioners have recognized the great importance of developing valid criteria and understanding their role in organizations. Consistent with this observation is the fact that all the HR functions to be discussed in the remainder of the text depend completely on adequate criteria.

In this chapter, the criterion problem was discussed at length and identified as a potential stumbling block to advancing research in I/O psychology. The measurement of performance criteria is as complex as it is important, which is why we speak of the criterion problem. Nevertheless, we are making progress in the process of presenting generally accepted definitions of criteria, examples of criteria, and evaluative standards for criteria, such as relevance, reliability, sensitivity, practicality, and fairness. The ultimate criterion and the actual criterion were defined and discussed, and the traditional view of criteria was explained in detail; also discussed were more recent concerns about the impression that this view can give about the nature of criteria. An actual criterion that does not cover a representative sample of the ultimate criterion was described as deficient, and one that measures things other than what is in the ultimate criterion was described as contaminated.

In discussing the criterion problem, the chapter highlighted two major issues that contribute to that problem. First, the debate regarding multiple criteria versus a composite criterion was considered; the text suggested that even though, from an applied perspective, a decision needs to be made based on some score or number, the variety of information that comes from using multiple criteria must not be ignored. Performance is surely multidimensional, and multiple criteria are needed to measure it well. Campbell's work in the area of performance modeling and approaches to criteria was highlighted as providing a model for how to proceed in this arena (Campbell, 1990; Campbell et al., 1993). Second, the common belief that criteria are dynamic was addressed. Indeed, a number of studies have provided support for the notion that an individual's performance changes over time. Issues of measurement and prediction were also considered in this context.

The differences between objective and subjective criteria were also examined, and attention was given to various examples of each (e.g., measures of productivity, absenteeism, and lateness) as well as to supervisor ratings of employees' performance. (The latter are discussed in the next chapter.) In addition, the chapter presented a newer component of performance criteria called contextual performance and considered a great deal of recent research in this area, identifying the various antecedents of contextual performance and considering this new line of work within an international context. Lastly, counterproductive work behaviors were also discussed as behaviors that have a negative impact on the organization and other employees. This discussion identified both antecedents of CWBs and their relationships with other organizational behaviors and potential spillover to other coworkers.

TEACHING THE CHAPTER

Defining criteria and describing important standards with which to assess a criterion are the key issues addressed in this chapter. In the first part of the chapter, students are presented with a description of the criterion problem to highlight the difficulty that is inherent in determining how to measure individual, organizational, or process-oriented performance.

The first exercise brings the issue of criteria selection to the forefront through a discussion of grading procedures used in elementary, secondary, and undergraduate coursework. Specifically, you will lead a discussion with your class about the criteria used in academic settings to measure success—*GRADES!* While only brave-hearted instructors may choose to have a class discussion on this issue, the conversation will give students insight into how instructors select criteria for performance. Most students should be able to easily relate to this issue, as they should be to some extent experts at being students and adapting to academic environments. Help your students apply this experience to emphasize some of the major points about criteria that are presented in this chapter.

The last part of the chapter distinguishes between objective and subjective criteria. It also introduces contextual performance, including counterproductive behavior. The next chapter is focused on performance appraisal and will present many more opportunities to examine objective and subjective criteria. However, in this chapter you may want to discuss contextual performance in greater detail as it is becoming a larger part of what I/O psychologists consider when designing selection, performance appraisal, and training programs. In the section that follows, a group simulation exercise is outlined. It may be a fun way for students to observe and think about the effects of contextual performance-related behaviors on perceptions of objective performance and performance criteria in the workplace.

While this is one of the shorter chapters of the book, it has been placed carefully so that it sets up the remaining chapters on performance appraisal, selection, and training.

SUGGESTED EXERCISES AND ASSIGNMENTS

College Course Criteria Selection

Purpose The main objective of this exercise is to stimulate students' discussion of the criterion problem by using their firsthand experiences with course grades. Note that this activity can prompt critiques of assignments or grading within the current course; instructors who want to use this activity should be prepared to address student critiques of grading procedures by providing a clear rationale. While this activity can leave the instructor open to criticism, it is also good for students to know that instructors put careful thought into evaluation procedures.

Instructions

- Divide students into small groups to generate responses to the following questions:
  - What is the ultimate criterion within the context of a college education?
  - In your college classes, what criteria have been most often used in evaluating your performance?
  - In your opinion, were these criteria highly relevant to the ultimate criterion?
  - Do you agree with how academic performance is assessed in college? If not, what would you use as actual criteria?
  - What is the best way to go about determining "good" criteria in an academic setting?
- Ask each group to share their answers with the class to generate conversations about how grades are determined, as well as what alternatives exist, and to gather your students' opinions on this issue.

Discussion Questions

- To what extent do you feel the criteria for this class are relevant to the ultimate criterion?
- To what extent are you aware of the grading criteria used in your classes?
- How do you use this awareness to enhance your class performance?

Instructor Evaluations

Purpose The main objective of this exercise is to provide students with a concrete example of how performance is measured and to give them an opportunity to critique it.

Instructions

- Obtain copies of the measure your institution uses to evaluate instructor performance.
- Divide students into small groups to generate responses to the following questions:
  - What items measure information unrelated to instructor performance (i.e., criterion contamination)?
  - What items might you add that you believe are missing (i.e., criterion deficiency)?
  - What else might be important to measure to assess a professor's/instructor's performance unrelated to classroom performance (e.g., research or service work)?
- Ask each group to share their answers to generate a discussion about problems and concerns they have with the measure.

Discussion Questions

- Do you believe students provide honest and accurate ratings on this form? Why or why not?
- How do you believe these ratings should be used? Is it appropriate to use these to determine which professors should receive promotions or be allowed to keep their jobs? Why or why not?

Job Analysis and Criteria Development

Purpose This exercise allows students to apply their job analysis data completed from the exercise in Chapter 3 and engage in identification of criteria.

Instructions

- *Prior to class:* If this exercise is to be conducted during class time, ask students to bring a copy of their job analysis to class. This activity can also be given as a course assignment.
- Ask students to use the information they obtained during the job analysis to help them identify and define several criteria important for success on the job. The criteria should be clearly linked to job success and organizational value.
  - How are these criteria related to compensation or salary for this job?

- Have students share their criteria and why they identified them as important.
    - Through this discussion, students can hear different rationales for selecting criteria (e.g., most frequently performed behaviors, value of criteria to the organization). It is important for students to hear other perspectives on this issue in order to maximize their learning.

Discussion Questions

- How did you go about selecting the most important criteria?
- What seem to be the key considerations when selecting criteria for job success?
- Are the most important criteria associated with the employee's salary?
- Have you had any work experiences in which you were evaluated on criteria that had a high degree of relevance (i.e., overlap between the actual and ultimate criteria)?

Job Analysis and Contextual Performance

Purpose The main objective of this exercise is to have students apply their job analysis data and recognize contextual performance.

Instructions

- *Prior to class:* As in the previous exercise, ask students to bring a copy of their job analysis to class if this exercise will be conducted during class time.
- Have students identify at least one example for each of the five categories of contextual performance:
    1. Working with extra enthusiasm to get the job done
    2. Volunteering to do things that aren't formally part of the job; taking on extra responsibility
    3. Helping others with their jobs (sportsmanship or organizational courtesy)
    4. Meeting deadlines and complying with organizational rules and regulations (civic virtue or conscientiousness)
    5. Supporting or defending the organization for which the employee works
- Have students share their examples with one another. Then, as a class, use the discussion questions below to guide your conversation about contextual performance and how it is differentiated from task performance.

Discussion Questions

- How does contextual performance differ from task performance?
- Could contextual performance overlap with task performance? If so, how?
- Have you engaged in contextual performance at work? If so, what did you do?
- Do you think that contextual performance should be rewarded? Why or why not?
- What might be a consequence of using *only* contextual performance to judge performance?

Organizational Citizenship Behaviors (OCBs)

Purpose This exercise demonstrates how OCBs can affect work group performance and perception of an individual's performance.

Instructions

- *Prior to class:* While any group game can be used for this exercise, one that involves making decisions and identifying actions for survival is most conducive to illustrating the point of this exercise. Games involving a group that must decide what to do if they were stranded on a deserted island, lost in the mountains, or lost in the desert are suggested examples.
  - Generate a list of steps or items that will enable the group to survive. Provide copies of the list to all group members.
  - For each role listed below, write the instructions for the role on a separate piece of paper to be given to a designated group member.
    - *Participant 1:* You are concerned with time pressure and need to focus only on keeping the team on task and making decisions as quickly as possible. Do not contribute much to the discussion of the issues. Instead, frequently mention that time is important for survival.
    - *Participant 2* (this individual will receive the correct rankings of the top five or so items for survival): Your role is to provide the group with the correct answers and do so without showing any consideration for the views of your team. You know the right answers (but do not be too obvious about that fact with your teammates), so you are not interested in discussing ideas. Instead, you just want the team to agree with your decisions—the less discussion and explanation, the better.
    - *Participant 3:* You are focused only on OCBs. You should not add anything of value to the discussion of the rankings of the items. However, you should spend the meeting time ensuring that everyone is "doing all right." Specifically, you should be helpful to others, provide encouragement and support, stick up for others, and volunteer to do anything for the group based on its decisions. However, be careful not to contribute any ideas to the actual decision making that takes place.
    - *Participant 4:* You are to be actively involved in the task, but watch out for someone who acts like a "know-it-all." If other participants try to dominate the decision-making process by acting like they have all the answers, be sure to step in and question everything those individuals say.
- *In class:* Select four volunteers to participate in a group role-play.
  - Explain the goal of the exercise to the volunteer group: to rank the items on the list (hand out the list of items) that will facilitate the group's survival while stranded.
  - Explain that the two criteria critical for success are: (1) speed of decision making and (2) decision-making accuracy (ability to correctly rank the items).

- Hand out the role instructions (prepared in a previous step) to the volunteers and instruct them to play their designated roles to the best of their ability. Also, you may want to instruct each volunteer not to share his or her role with the other team members.
- Tell the group they will have eight minutes to play the game and to work on their list. Begin timing the exercise as soon as the group begins discussion.
- Tell the rest of the class to observe the group and be ready to evaluate each member's performance on a scale of 1 (least effective) to 9 (highly effective) on the following criteria:
  - Contribution to the group goal of survival
  - Effort
  - Cooperation
  - Leadership
  - Anything else that seems relevant to group performance
- After the role-play has concluded, have the class rank the performance of each group member. This exercise is intended to result in Participant 3 (the OCBer) being rated very highly even though he or she contributed very little to the group goal of successful survival decisions.
- Be sure to explain to the class the prescribed roles of each volunteer participant.

Discussion Questions

- Why did the OCB participant receive such high ratings (if relevant to the class's ratings)?
- What other criteria were used in evaluating the performance of the participants?
- What might the findings in our simulation say about how employee evaluations are made in organizations?
- Are there other criteria that we could have used in order to obtain greater accuracy and fairness in our ratings?

EVALUATING "TAKING IT TO THE FIELD"

The Chapter 4 activity involves providing a critique of metrics used to assess performance among gardeners. This activity is intended to get students thinking about some of the difficulties associated with defining and measuring criteria. As such, the important part of this assignment is that students be effective in critiquing the current metrics provided by Stacia. Students who simply state that all the metrics are adequate are not thinking carefully about why certain metrics might be different among gardeners.

Below are some potential responses you may receive from students.

Poor responses...	■ Demonstrate little critical thinking (e.g., "Your performance measures are great!"). ■ Fail to specifically discuss each potential performance measure. ■ Fail to provide Stacia with any potential new performance measure metrics.
Good responses...	■ Demonstrate that the student has carefully considered what each metric may measure. The student should explain to Stacia some of the more obvious shortcomings of each metric. For example, students could note that some clients may want certain plants even if they die easily; if these plants fail to survive, it may not be the fault of the gardener. ■ Provide reasonably effective suggestions for measuring performance, such as supervisor evaluations, peer evaluations, and the like.
Excellent responses...	■ Demonstrate that the student has carefully considered what each metric measures. Students should explain to Stacia some of the more complex shortcomings of the measures (e.g., some plants may be more vulnerable to diseases and insect infestations in particular geographic regions). ■ Provide effective and interesting suggestions for measuring performance, such as how much profit the gardener generates, how many new contracts the gardener sells each year, and so on.

Possible Critiques

Number of plants that die: The number of plant deaths may not necessarily indicate the gardener's skill. For example, some clients ask for plants that are difficult to care for; some clients have children or pets that kill the plants; drought, disease, or other problems can also cause plants to die. Furthermore, larger plants (e.g., trees) may be more serious problems if they die, compared to smaller plants (e.g., tulips).

Number of houses visited per week: Some large properties may take a long time to care for; gardeners who visit a large number of houses per week may be doing poor-quality work; if gardeners are in an area where clients are more separated (e.g., rural areas) or where traffic is difficult (e.g., populous urban areas), it may take them a long time to get from one client to another.

Satisfaction ratings from the gardener's customer: Skilled gardeners may not always be well liked by their clients; clients may also have unreasonable expectations or may imply they are dissatisfied in the hope that they will receive discounts or compensation.

EVALUATING "APPLICATION QUESTIONS"

1. Consider some of the ways your performance as a student is evaluated (e.g., exams, papers, projects). What might be some examples of criterion deficiency (i.e., what are some aspects of student performance that are not well assessed using these types of measures)? What might be some examples of criterion contamination (i.e., what are some aspects students might be judged on that are not relevant to student performance)?

   Evaluation Guide: Students are apt to come up with a number of examples for this. If you have a group of students who have more work experience, you can tailor this question to discuss their experiences in the workplace as well and contrast how work performance measures differ from exams and papers students complete in school. Common responses may include the following points:
   - Criterion deficiency may include aspects of performance that teachers are unable to observe, such as time spent studying, time spent helping and mentoring other students, time spent on schoolwork despite having important personal concerns or tragedies, and individual effort put forth on group projects.
   - Criterion contamination may exist when teachers display favoritism toward students they like or when teachers give lower grades to students who don't share their opinion or students who experience test anxiety.
   - This question may lead to some interesting discussions that can help students understand the instructor's position on some issues. For example, you might ask students to consider a professor who will not let students hand in papers if they are unstapled or not printed on time: Is that a valid measure of performance? Why or why not? Discussing issues that might get in the way of accurately assessing someone's knowledge (test anxiety, being ill) could also prove interesting.

2. In the United States, there is a great deal of debate about how to distinguish good teachers from poor teachers in public schools. Some people advocate using student scores on standardized tests to determine which teachers are doing well. Other people advocate using student ratings of teachers. What are some pros and cons of each approach?

   Evaluation Guide: This is a particularly complex issue, and students will likely have strong and varied opinions about the topic. Here are some potential issues that might come up:
   - Using standardized test scores to determine which teachers are doing well has a number of advantages; for example, using such scores makes it easier to compare teachers across schools, and they are easy to operationalize and measure. One problem with this approach is that some teachers may have more resources than others as well as students with different ability levels, making it appear as though there is a difference in teaching when it is actually

a difference in student performance. Other potential problems are that teachers will teach to the test or that cheating will occur to ensure good test scores.

■ Using student ratings has a number of benefits as well. Student ratings can indicate how enjoyable and engaged the instructor is, and they are easy to measure. Some potential problems are that when students are having fun, they are not necessarily learning the content; that students who receive poor grades may retaliate by giving poor evaluations; and that some teachers in unpopular subject areas, such as math, might be penalized unfairly.

3. What are some examples of contextual performance that you might have engaged in at your job or in your classes? When were you most likely to perform those behaviors? Did they ever get in the way of your task performance?

   Evaluation Guide: Students will likely name a number of behaviors, including speaking favorably of their organization, helping coworkers with difficult tasks, or cleaning up communal areas. Possible discussions might include the following issues:

   ■ Students tend to be more likely to engage in contextual behaviors when they have time, feel confident they will be successful in helping others, and like their organization. You could discuss how organizational climate and the way in which work is organized might prompt employees to engage in more of these behaviors.

   ■ You could also discuss whether these behaviors are really part of performance if they are not explicitly stated in the job description, examining some of the advantages to considering them as performance (encourages people to perform these behaviors; gives people credit for taking time out of their day to help) and some of the disadvantages (busier people may not have as much time for such behavior; if they are not required, it is unfair to use them in performance reviews).

   ■ Finally, the book noted that with contextual performance/OCBs, there is such a thing as "too much as a good thing" and task performance can suffer. Prompt students to think of times this might occur, such as staying up late to help a friend and then sleeping through their own class, or spending too much time doing volunteer activities and failing to complete their homework. Encourage them to think about how they might find a good balance between helping out, which may have a positive effect for them, and learning to say "no" when it will negatively affect them.

4. Imagine that you have a subordinate who has shared something negative about one of his clients using social media (e.g., on Twitter or Facebook). Do you believe this behavior is a part of performance that should be considered during his performance review? Why or why not?

   Evaluation Guide: This thought experiment may help students consider their own behaviors from the point of view of a supervisor. Some topics to discuss might include the following:

   ■ Is it appropriate to consider things an employee does outside of work as part of job performance? On the one hand, employers cannot dictate what employees can do outside the workplace; on the other hand, sharing something like this can have important ramifications at work, on coworkers, and on how that person is regarded in the organization.

- What might be some consequences at work if colleagues or clients see the insulting post?
- What are some more appropriate and constructive ways for employees to "vent" when they are frustrated with their jobs or clients?

HIGHLIGHTED STUDY FOR DISCUSSION

Sackett, P. R., Zedeck, S., & Fogli, L. (1988). Relations between measures of typical and maximum job performance. *Journal of Applied Psychology, 73*, 482–486.

This article helped to demonstrate the importance of understanding the difference between typical and maximum performance in the selection context. Although this is a relatively dated article, it is clearly written and includes measures that are easily understood by most students. It is also quite short and manageable, even for students who have little experience reading articles from scholarly journals. Key points in the article include the following:

- Maximum performance occurs when (1) subjects know they are being evaluated, (2) subjects recognize (either implicitly or explicitly) that they are to attempt to maximize their performance, and (3) measurement of performance takes place over a relatively short time. Typical performance, in contrast, occurs when these conditions are not present and better reflects how individuals are apt to perform most of the time.
- Comparing typical and maximum performance has important implications for understanding why different measures of performance may not converge if they measure different types of performance.
- Participants in the study were store cashiers. Maximum performance was measured by having the participants scan 25 standard items from shopping carts as quickly as possible; this was tested by scanning items from two of these shopping carts one after another, and then again after 15 days. Typical performance was assessed by measuring items scanned per minute and the accuracy of scans over the course of four weeks.
- Results indicated that typical and maximal performance demonstrate only moderate correlations with each other (.16 in one sample and .36 in another). This suggests that measures of maximal versus typical performance assess different constructs. This finding presents an excellent opportunity to discuss some problems that might occur with certain selection measures (e.g., just because someone does well on a job simulation does not necessarily predict that that person will have high typical performance). Students can be encouraged to think of times they have been measured on typical versus maximum performance and to discuss how these performances differed for them.

WEB LEARNING

Title	Address
Academy of Management Journal	http://aom.org/amj/
Academy of Management: Research Methods Division	http://division.aomonline.org/rm/joomla
O*NET	http://online.onetcenter.org
Statistics for Psychologists: Resources on the web	http://www.psychwww.com/resource/bytopic/stats.html
American Statistical Association (ASA)	http://www.amstat.org
Principles for the Validation and Use of Personnel Selection Procedures, 4th edition	http://www.siop.org/_Principles/principles.pdf
Counterproductive Behavior at Work	http://chuma.cas.usf.edu/~spector/counterpage.html

Performance Appraisal

Chapter Summary

Performance appraisals are used to make personnel decisions, to provide employees with important job-related feedback, and to document employee performance as a way of protecting the organization from potential legal suits. Industrial/organizational psychologists often play an active and important role in the performance management systems of organizations.

Performance appraisals are available in many formats, including graphic rating scales, BARS, CARS, checklists, and employee comparison procedures. Each format has advantages and disadvantages (see Table 5.1); none have clearly been identified as the single best approach. The process of appraising an individual's performance is very complex and can result in rating errors such as halo, leniency, central tendency, and severity. Two types of rater training, Rater Error Training (RET) and Frame of Reference (FOR) Training, have been established as potentially useful in reducing these errors and/or improving accuracy.

Contemporary performance appraisal research continues to focus on the social-psychological context in which the appraisal takes place. This research indicates that ratee and rater reactions toward the appraisal process are important in measuring the success of an appraisal system. Also relevant to the appraisal process are the relationship between the supervisor and subordinate, the political climate within the organization, the rater's motivation and accountability, and the degree of trust among raters.

Participation is another integral element in the appraisal process. One interesting development in this area is the 360-degree feedback system, in which employees receive performance feedback from peers, subordinates, supervisors, and clients/customers. Self-ratings are commonly included in this system, especially when the only other participant is the supervisor. Although 360-degree feedback is relatively new, research indicates not only that many employees like it but also that it has a great deal of potential for improving the feedback process in general. Employee development continues to grow in importance as both employees and organizations recognize the benefits of employee growth and learning. Employee development not only benefits individual workers but also functions as a source of competitive advantage for organizations that encourage and provide opportunities for development.

Adherence to legal guidelines is also critical to the performance appraisal process. Recent work has identified fairness as important not only to ratees but also to the courts, which appear to weight it quite heavily in making judgments for or against plaintiffs. And while emerging technology, such as wearables, will lead to many interesting and innovative approaches to performance management, it may also raise legal concerns over privacy violations.

As we have seen, performance appraisal has widespread implications for organizations because appraisal information is used for such important personnel decisions as promotions, demotions, layoffs, dismissals, and raises. Obviously, invalid performance appraisal information is likely to result in poor organizational decisions. Our understanding of the appraisal process is thus enhanced by our appreciation of the context in which it takes place.

TEACHING THE CHAPTER

The concept of criterion development in Chapter 4 is directly applied and reinforced in Chapter 5 by considering issues regarding the design and implementation of performance appraisals. The purposes of performance appraisal are discussed, with emphasis on its ability to collect data for personnel decisions, employee development, and documentation of employee performance to protect against legal action. The material in Chapter 5 also lends itself to applying data from the job analysis assignment given earlier in the course in Chapter 3. Specifically, the first activity involves creating a performance appraisal format that best evaluates performance.

This is a relatively comprehensive chapter and can be somewhat difficult to teach; numerous facets of the appraisal process are covered, so there is a lot of material to cover. If you have access to sample performance appraisals that use different types of rating formats, it might be helpful to bring these to class to give students a better understanding of what performance appraisals look like in the real world.

You might want to devote an entire class period to reviewing student performance appraisals. During the review, you should discuss the extent to which students' job analyses and the chapter information facilitated their ability to complete the assignment. When students apply their job analysis to other projects, they often find that they might have approached it differently (e.g., sought different information or covered other areas of the job). However, the lessons students learn can be quite interesting and can contribute to effective classroom discussion.

SUGGESTED EXERCISES AND ASSIGNMENTS

Performance Appraisal Development

Purpose In this exercise, students apply previously generated job analysis data and use this information to create a performance appraisal instrument.

Instructions This assignment contains two parts: (1) rater instructions for the appraisal of the target job and (2) development of an abbreviated performance appraisal.

Part I: Rater Instructions Students should consider some of the problems that occur (i.e., rating errors) when evaluating performance, the legal issues related to performance appraisal, and how their performance appraisal instrument is designed to minimize error and improve accuracy. These instructions should address the following questions:

- How often are subordinates evaluated?
- What types of rating scales are used and why?
- What behaviors are most relevant to the appraisal?
- How often should the rater collect performance information?
- What can the rater do to minimize the chances of creating biased ratings?
- How does this system address any potential legal concerns?

Part II: Performance Appraisal Instrument Students should revisit the criteria they identified in the Chapter 4 assignment "Job Analysis and Criteria Development" and select two to four criteria. For each criterion (or dimension), they should create a rating scale (with a format type of their choosing). The instrument should address the following questions:

- Does the instrument focus on results or behaviors?
- To what degree are the criteria subjective or objective? What advantages or disadvantages do they present for the appraisal's effectiveness?
- Are the scales easy to use (from a rater's point of view)? Do they differentiate between high- and low-performing individuals?
- Does putting the criteria (or dimensions) in performance appraisal format affect how ratings are made?

Discussion Questions

- Describe your ratings scale. What issues did you consider when you were designing your measure?
- What might be some strengths and weaknesses of your scale?
- Do you believe your raters would answer accurately on your scale? Why or why not?

Performance Appraisal in the Courtroom

Purpose The objective of this exercise is to make students aware of the consequences of poorly designed/implemented performance appraisal systems.

Instructions Either have students identify a legal case involving a performance appraisal system *or* designate a particular legal case for them to review. Students should research the case and then write and turn in a summary of the case. Alternatively, this assignment could be carried out in a variety of other ways—class discussion, class presentation, take-home assignment, or a combination of these methods. The written summary and/or class presentation should include the following:

- Who was the plaintiff in the case? Who was the defendant?
- What was the main reason why the plaintiff sued the defendant?
- Describe the performance appraisal that was used by the defendant.
- Who created the performance appraisal? The defendant or an outside company? Did this make a difference?
- Was a job analysis mentioned?
- How did the court rule in this case? What was the outcome?
- What is your opinion on this case? Do you agree with the verdict and the outcome for the winning party?
- What might be some challenges associated with implementing a new performance appraisal system in this organization?
- What could you do to establish trust between the organization and its employees with regard to the performance appraisal system?

Discussion Questions

- Have you ever experienced a performance appraisal you thought was unfair or illegal? What was the system? Why was it problematic?
- Were there any parts of the legal case that surprised you? Why?
- Do you think the final verdict was fair? Why or why not?

Current Research in Performance Appraisal

Purpose The objective of this exercise is to make students aware of current research issues in performance appraisal.

Instructions Either have students identify a recent (within the last five years) research article related to a contemporary issue in performance appraisal research *or* designate a particular research article for them to review. Students should review the article and then write and turn in a summary of the article. Alternatively, you could distribute copies of the article to the class (depending on the size of your class) to facilitate an in-class discussion. Here is a list of suggested journals from which to choose an article:

- *Journal of Applied Psychology*
- *Personnel Psychology*
- *Academy of Management Journal*
- *Journal of Management*
- *Organizational Behavior and Human Decision Processes*

Students should answer the following questions about the article:

- What year was the article published?
- Who is/are the author(s)?
- What are the hypotheses?
- What type of research method was used?
- What did the author(s) find?
- How does this article relate to the social-psychological context?
- What are the implications of this research for organizations?

Discussion Questions

- How might an organization use the findings in the article to improve their performance appraisal system?
- What are some weaknesses or flaws in the study? How might researchers address this weakness in a future study?
- If you were a researcher, what hypotheses would you propose for a future study?

Examining Rater Errors

Purpose The objective of this exercise is to provide a concrete example of how raters use rating scales, mistakes they make, and ways these mistakes can be prevented.

Instructions

- *Prior to class:* Design a survey for assessing your teaching performance. The measure should include a number of constructs students have had an opportunity to observe (e.g., speaks with a clear voice; presentation quality; provides helpful examples) and some that students have not likely observed (e.g., works well with colleagues, conducts rigorous research, engages in professional development). You might also incorporate some items over which you have no control (e.g., having to do with the quality of the classroom, the size of the class, the time the class is offered).
- If you have a relatively large class (40+ students), you could introduce a manipulation, telling some students that the evaluation is to help you develop as a professor and others that it will be used to determine whether you will be rehired/allowed to teach the I/O course again.

- Distribute this assessment before the day you intend to discuss performance appraisal so you have enough time to collect and analyze student responses. You will likely find the following responses:
  - In general, if you performed the manipulation mentioned above, students who received a version implying that their feedback will affect your job status will be more lenient in their ratings than students who believe the ratings will be used for development purposes.
  - Students also typically provide ratings for items they have not actually observed. These ratings often reflect either halo or central tendency errors.
- Provide students with an overview of some of your ratings. You can break down the overview by question, or you can divide it into ratings of items students have and have not been able to observe.

Discussion Questions
- You likely had a hard time answering some of these items because you have never observed your instructor using these skills. On what did you base your ratings? How is this relevant to performance appraisal?
- Consider a website such as www.ratemyprofessor.com. Do you think these ratings truly reflect professors' performance? Who is likely to evaluate professors on this site?

Developing BARS to Evaluate Customer Service

Purpose The objective of this exercise is to give students experience in developing a type of appraisal format and to see firsthand the benefits and drawbacks of using the behaviorally anchored rating scale (BARS) format.

Instructions
- Divide the class into groups of four to six.
- Have students create a 9-point BARS for evaluating a retail salesperson, where 1 is low effectiveness and 9 is high effectiveness.
  - Step 1: Generate behavioral examples related to customer service. Students will likely have some horrific and some great stories that illustrate various levels of customer service they have experienced when shopping. These will serve as critical incidents and should illustrate extremely effective to extremely ineffective performance.
  - Step 2: Rate each example on effectiveness (1 is low, 9 is high).
  - Step 3: Have the group choose nine items as behavioral anchors for the final scale.
  - Step 4: Have the group draw their BARS so they can share it with other groups. A chalkboard or flipchart can be used to facilitate this step.

Discussion Questions
- Are there any noticeable differences between each group's scales?
- What are some common behaviors that appear on all the scales?

- Was it difficult to evaluate the behaviors on a continuum of effectiveness? Are there any numbers on your rating scale that do not have examples? If so, why do you think that is so?
- Do you think that your rating scale is a fair assessment of customer service? Why or why not?
- What are the main strengths and weaknesses of the scale you developed?

EVALUATING "TAKING IT TO THE FIELD"

In this activity, Pai Ng, a director of institutional research at a college, asks for feedback on a measure she uses to assess professors' performance and also asks what the BARS rating system is all about. Student responses are likely to vary widely on this assignment. Below are some possible guidelines for grading student responses.

Poor responses...	■ Fail to demonstrate careful thought about the items on the measure (e.g., "Your evaluation looks great the way it is!").
	■ Fail to provide specific or clear suggestions for Pai.
	■ Overlook the possibility that Pai could use an alternative format for her evaluation (e.g., the possibility of open-ended questions, BARS, etc.).
	■ Offer impractical solutions (e.g., rater training for all students).
Good responses...	■ Note that the scale she uses fails to capture negative responses.
	■ Note areas of criterion deficiency (e.g., an item measuring the instructor's speaking skills would be a reasonable suggestion).
	■ Note areas of criterion contamination (e.g., instructors do not have control over the room they teach in or whether students come to class).
	■ Provide some suggestions for additional questions; these suggestions should be carefully worded and should assess aspects that are relevant to teaching in a classroom (e.g., getting students involved, using class time effectively).
	■ Provide information on BARS and a suggestion as to whether Pai should use this instrument. Students can argue either way—BARS do help improve the accuracy of ratings, but they are also expensive and time-consuming to develop.

Excellent responses...

- Note that the scale she uses fails to capture negative responses.
- Note areas of criterion deficiency (e.g., an item measuring the instructor's speaking skills would be a reasonable suggestion).
- Note areas of criterion contamination (e.g., instructors do not have control over the room they teach in or whether students come to class).
- Indicate which items may be vaguely worded (e.g., what is meant by "responses to e-mails"? By "timeliness"? By "quality"?).
- Address whether items are actually measuring what they are intended to measure (e.g., whether the class was interesting may depend on whether it is in the students' majors; whether students liked the instructor, or felt the grading was fair may be affected by their grade in the course). Particularly strong responses may note that performance is about behaviors, and there are not many behaviors assessed in this measure.
- Provide feedback for the last item—because it implies that their feedback may be used to lay off an instructor, students will tend to be lenient on this item.
- Provide some suggestions for additional questions; these suggestions should be carefully worded and should assess aspects that are relevant to teaching in a classroom (e.g., getting students involved; using class time effectively).
- Provide information on BARS and an illustrative example as well as a suggestion as to whether Pai should use this instrument. Students can argue either way—BARS do help improve the accuracy of ratings, but they are also expensive and time-consuming to develop.

EVALUATING "APPLICATION QUESTIONS"

1. Imagine that when using a 360-degree performance appraisal system, an employee receives a rating of 3.5/5 from his supervisor, 4.2/5 from his peers, and 2.25/5 from his subordinates. What might be some reasons for these discrepancies? What would you recommend that this individual's supervisor do to gain a better understanding of what these ratings indicate about the employee's performance?

Evaluation Guide: Students should note that the differences in ratings could be due to rater error or could reflect actual differences in that employee's skill in dealing with different groups of people. Some points to consider:

- Students might note the discrepancy between the supervisor's and the peers' ratings. First, this difference may be due to rater errors. For example, the supervisor might not be around to observe some of this employee's skill in negotiating and working with his peers. Alternatively, perhaps this individual's peers are providing lenient ratings because they don't want to hurt their relationships with him. These differences may also reflect meaningful differences in his performance; perhaps he is quite effective at managing teamwork but not very effective at higher-level functions or functions that are more related to the organization's goals (which would be more relevant to the supervisor).

- Students might also note the discrepancy between the high supervisor/ peer ratings and the low subordinate ratings. Once again, this could be due to rater error—perhaps the subordinates are upset about a policy change or some of the work they are completing and are retaliating by providing harsh ratings. Alternatively, perhaps these ratings reflect a meaningful performance issue—maybe the subordinates know that this person is incompetent, and they constantly need to fix his work (and his supervisor is not aware of this issue). Perhaps this employee is also abusive or unreasonable toward his subordinates, a fact he hides from his peers and supervisor.

- In terms of next steps, students should indicate that more information would be helpful. For example, the supervisor could solicit ratings on what parts of his performance are adequate and inadequate, meet with the raters to learn more about the reasoning behind their ratings, or meet with the employee to see if he has thoughts on why his ratings are different. Students may also suggest that it would be helpful to ensure that all parties are using the rating scale in the same way in case the differences are due to rater errors. Students may also suggest incorporating technology in interesting ways, including more frequent ratings, using online surveys to collect information, or providing online training modules to help people use the rating scales more accurately.

2. Imagine that, in order to assign grades on a group project, your professor requires all group members to provide ratings for one another, which he will consider in grading the project. One group member has been particularly troublesome— she has been argumentative, refuses to accommodate other group members' schedules, and completes the bare minimum amount of work. Would you feel comfortable giving her a poor performance appraisal? Why or why not?

Evaluation Guide: This scenario often evokes considerable interest among students, as most of them have had some frustrating experiences with group projects. Whether students would be comfortable giving this student a low score is a subjective issue, but some potential discussion topics might include the following:

- If students are unwilling to give this student a poor rating, ask them why it is difficult to do so. Students may indicate that they would have concerns about the rating affecting their own grades, that they don't want to make this person mad (and perhaps even more difficult), or that they feel badly about the consequence this might have on her grades. You could further prompt students to consider why it might be important for the professor to know about problems with this group member.

- If students say they would give the student a low rating, ask them what grade they would give the student. In many cases, students are willing to give a poor grade (C) but not a failing one. This may lead to further discussion about the difficulty in giving honest feedback when you know it may have a serious consequence (e.g., getting someone fired).
- It might also be fruitful to discuss what students could do to avoid the situation (e.g., talk to the teacher ahead of time, have a feedback session with the problematic student).

3. Once again, imagine that your professor has asked for your feedback on your fellow group members' performance on a project. This time, you have a group member who is very proactive in volunteering and takes an active role; however, even though she tries very hard, she has a lot of trouble understanding concepts introduced in the class; as a result, often the work she does is not usable for the project. Would you feel comfortable giving her a poor performance appraisal? Why or why not?

   Evaluation Guide: This can sometimes be a tough discussion for students, as they likely feel some sympathy for this student but also recognize that her performance is not effective. Potential discussion topics include the following:
   - If students are unwilling to give this student a poor grade, discuss why that might be. It is possible that they want to give her credit for her effort. If this is the case, have them discuss some of the eventual consequences of giving her an acceptable rating when her performance is not acceptable.
   - If students do decide to give this student a low rating, discuss some steps that can be taken to help her do a better job. For example, students might suggest switching around tasks in the group to give this student simpler tasks that she can perform more effectively or having another student work with her to help her when she is struggling. Students may also suggest ways of getting support from the instructor to help them with this student.

4. In many work environments, employees can engage in organizational citizenship behaviors (acts that help coworkers or the organization, even though they are not part of their job), such as staying late to work on a project they are not normally a part of or speaking positively about the organization to other people. Should these behaviors be considered in a performance appraisal? Why or why not?

   Evaluation Guide: Although the concept of contextual performance/OCBs was covered in Chapter 4, it is often helpful to reconsider it when discussing performance evaluation, as the realities of having contextual performance incorporated into performance measures are not always immediately evident. Students often make a snap judgment on this topic without thinking through the implications. Consider addressing the following issues:
   - If employees are now required to do "extra" things like helping other teams and speaking well about the organization, what might be some effects on

employee morale? Who will be more excited about this type of change, employees who feel connected to the company or employees who feel frustrated by the company?

- If employees are required to do "extra" things, how will that change what a person thinks and feels when someone else does something extra?
- What are some other ways in which OCBs can be recognized outside of a performance appraisal context? Awards, certificates, or other recognition ceremonies might be one approach students can consider.

5. Think of a time when you worked with someone who did not perform as well as you believed he or she should. What sorts of things did this person do/not do that led to a poor performance? If you were asked to deliver feedback to this person, what would you say?

Evaluation Guide: Student responses will vary a great deal on this question. However, keep in mind the following points as you discuss this issue:

- Effective feedback should be focused on the individual's behavior, not on the individual him- or herself. For example, a student should not say "I would tell this student he needed to stop being so lazy"—a better response would be "I would tell this student that when he is late to meetings, it makes it difficult for our group to get our work completed on time."
- Although students have not learned about justice theory yet, you can incorporate pieces of this concept into your discussion—for example, emphasizing the importance of being respectful and providing specific examples and information about the problematic behavior.

HIGHLIGHTED STUDY FOR DISCUSSION

As an alternative to an empirical study, a series of three blog posts by Rod McCloy and Andrea Sinclair of HumRRO are the topic for discussion. These posts examine the difficult question of teacher evaluation and ask why I/O psychologists have not played a larger part in the debate. These three series can be reviewed in class individually or together:

Part 1: Performance or Effectiveness? A Critical Distinction for Teacher Evaluation: http://blogs.edweek.org/edweek/on_performance/2011/10/performance_or_effectiveness_a_critical_distinction_for_teacher_evaluation.html

Part 2: Ramifications of the Performance/Effectiveness Distinction for Teacher Evaluation: http://blogs.edweek.org/edweek/on_performance/2011/11/ramifications_of_the_performanceeffectiveness_distinction_for_teacher_evaluation.html

Part 3: Recommendations for Developing Teacher Evaluation Systems: http://blogs.edweek.org/edweek/on_performance/2011/11/recommendations_for_developing_teacher_evaluation_systems.html

- In Part 1, the authors discuss the controversy over teaching evaluations and introduce the concept of I/O psychology. They provide a definition of performance and emphasize that it is not the same thing as effectiveness. The authors then argue that using standardized test scores (a measure of effectiveness) rather than a performance measure (an evaluation of teacher behaviors) can cause a number of problems. They particularly focus on the idea that some issues are not under teacher control and thus are not something the teacher can change.
- In Part 2, the authors are more specific about why measuring effectiveness, not performance, is problematic. Specifically, high-performing teachers may not be effective, teachers who are effective in one location may not be effective in another, and focusing on performance can ultimately lead to effectiveness. The authors also discuss shortcomings of value-added modeling (VAM).
- In Part 3, the authors provide several suggestions for evaluating teachers, which include the following:
  - Creating comprehensive, multidimensional performance measures
  - Keeping performance and effectiveness ratings separate and evaluating only on performance (not effectiveness)
  - Realizing that teachers perform other tasks in addition to classroom teaching, such as motivating students, managing dangerous students, and the like

WEB LEARNING

Title	Address
U.S. Office of Personnel Management: Performance Management	http://www.opm.gov/perform/overview.asp
Online HR Guide: Performance Appraisal and 360-Degree Feedback Forms	http://www.hr-guide.com/data/133.htm
Online HR Guide: Manager's Guide to Performance Appraisal	http://www.hr-guide.com/data/132.htm
Society for Human Resource Management (SHRM)	http://www.shrm.org
Links to 360-Degree Feedback websites	http://www.hr-software.net/pages/215.htm
Performance Management and Appraisal Resource Center	http://performance-appraisals.org/
Community for Human Resource Management (CHRM)	http://www.chrmglobal.com/index.php
Links to Performance Appraisal Software	http://www.hr-guide.com/data/209.htm

CHAPTER 6

Predictors

LEARNING OBJECTIVES

This chapter should help students understand:

- The definition of a test and how to find existing tests used for personnel selection

- The difference between various testing formats, such as speed versus power tests, individual versus group tests, and paper-and-pencil versus performance tests

- The importance of validity coefficients to employee selection

- Definitions, estimates of validity, and examples of the following types of predictors: cognitive ability (both general and specific) tests, psychomotor tests, personality tests, integrity tests, work samples, assessment centers, biographical information, and interviews

Chapter Summary

In this chapter, tests were classified in terms of form (e.g., pencil-and-paper) as well as the predictor type (e.g., cognitive ability) they represent. The most frequently used selection instruments—cognitive ability tests, psychomotor tests, personality tests, integrity tests, work sample tests, ACs, biographical information, and interviews— were discussed in the context of their role in employee selection. The validity coefficients of these selection instruments are listed in Table 6.5. Note that the variability of these coefficients may be due to the diversity of the studies included in the meta-analyses (e.g., Hunter & Hunter, 1984, versus Bertua et al., 2005) as well as to differences among the predictors and criteria.

We can draw a few general conclusions. First, it is clear that ability measures (e.g., general cognitive, specific cognitive, and psychomotor) are among the most valid predictors of performance criteria in an employment setting. Second, the validity coefficients for personality tests are not as high as those for most of the other predictors included in our review. Third, nontraditional predictors, such as integrity tests, biodata, work samples, and ACs, are consistently valid predictors of on-the-job performance. Finally, structured interviews tend to be better predictors of job performance than unstructured interviews. In Chapter 7, we will discuss the actual selection process, focusing also on the legalities involved in how organizations use these predictors to hire employees.

TEACHING THE CHAPTER

Selecting predictors along with designing assessments for applicant selection and employment evaluation are two of the most important applications of I/O psychology. This area of the field will be the most recognizable to most students, as they have likely been involved in filling out job applications, taking employment tests, and/or taking part in job interviews. It is particularly important to clearly convey the material in this chapter and to reinforce that predictors should be derived from the job analysis. The exercises and activities for this chapter were designed with this in mind. All of them require students either to apply their job analysis assignment from earlier in the course or to use the suggestions from Chapter 6 for providing explicit KSAO information when selecting predictors, designing applications, and developing questions for structured interviews.

When reviewing the different kinds of tests, note that the book uses the SAT and ACT as examples; students may want to contribute their own college entrance exam experiences. Further, if you are working with more senior students, you may want to facilitate a discussion around the GRE and its adaptation from paper-and-pencil format to a computer adaptive format. You may find http://www.gre.org to be a useful resource in guiding discussion on computer testing, especially with regard to the accuracy of these computerized tests.

You will notice that a considerable part of this chapter is dedicated to describing the different types of predictors used for selection purposes in organizations. As mentioned previously, students should have some familiarity with many of these predictors. Discussing and sharing these experiences with one another will likely be a valuable complement to the lecture on these topics. Conversations around students' experiences (good and bad) with interviews, integrity tests, and biodata may elicit some interesting stories. The majority of the exercises outlined below are designed to demonstrate the importance of using job analysis data as the starting point for predictor selection and assessment design.

SUGGESTED EXERCISES AND ASSIGNMENTS

Identifying Predictors

Purpose The objective of this exercise is for students to apply their job analysis data from the Chapter 3 exercise and to identify the most effective predictors to use when selecting a job candidate.

Instructions

- You might begin teaching the chapter with this exercise and then have students revisit their predictor choices from Chapter 3 after you have presented all of the predictors during the lecture.
- Students should have read the chapter before this class exercise, but they may need to use their book to help them identify and describe the predictors they

would select for their job. Alternatively, you can show a slide or provide a handout listing of all the possible predictors.

- Inform students that they are I/O psychologists hired by a company to develop a cost-effective method for selecting candidates for the job they analyzed (during the job analysis exercise). Because the company has limits on costs (time and money), they can choose only three types of predictors. Give students 10 minutes to do the following:
  - Review their job's KSAO list
  - Identify the three most effective predictors for selecting a candidate for their job and the rationale for these choices
  - Share their choices with classmates (individually or in groups)
- After you have discussed all the predictors outlined in the chapter, open up discussion on how students chose their predictors. Ask if they would make any changes to their three predictors based on what they have learned.
- To challenge students and engage them further, tell them they have to replace at least one of their predictors with a different one.
- As an out-of-class exercise, you might have students write up their three predictors and their rationales (based on the job and the characteristics of the predictors).

Discussion Questions

- What are the most frequently chosen predictors?
- Why were these predictors chosen over others?
- Which predictors were replaced and why?

Developing an Application Blank

Purpose The objective of this exercise is to have students design an application blank, apply their own experience, and learn the importance of using applications that are legally defensible.

Instructions

- Divide students into groups of four to six and have them select one student's job analysis data for this exercise. As an alternative, predetermine the job that will be used for this exercise (e.g., Customer Service Representative, O★NET code: 43-4051.00; Retail Sales Person, O★NET code: 41-2031.00).
- Have students refer to the KSAOs derived from the job analysis (or the O★NET) to guide this exercise.
- In their groups, have students design a 10- to 15-item application blank for the job. They should provide justification for each item they include on the application blank.

Discussion Questions

- What did you think were the most important KSAOs for selection?
- How did you select the items for your application blank? Was there any disagreement in your group about what to include on the application blank?

- Are all of your items legally defensible?
- Is there anything you wanted to include but could not defend?

Using Biodata to Hire an Auto Mechanic

Purpose Many students own a car, so they should have some firsthand knowledge about the importance of finding a good mechanic. In this exercise, students will apply their experiences to create biodata questions for the assessment of an auto mechanic.

Instructions

- *Prior to class:* Look up the O★NET description for auto mechanic at http://online.onetcenter.org (Automotive Body and Related Repairers, O★NET code: 49-3021.00).
- Have the entire class brainstorm approximately 10 KSAOs that define the job requirements, or refer to the O★NET information.
- Divide the class into as many groups as there are KSAOs for the job. Ask each group to generate five biodata items to use for selection purposes. Refer them to Table 6.3 for examples of biodata items for a customer service job.
- Have groups share their items and the rationales behind their use with the rest of the class. Facilitate the group presentations to ensure that they do not take up too much time. If you become short on time, you may want to have groups share only their best biodata items.

Discussion Questions

- Was creating these items harder or easier than you thought it would be?
- Would these items be perceived as valid by job applicants?
- Are these items content-valid?
- Would you hire an auto mechanic based on these biodata items alone?

Structured Interview Development

Purpose The objective of this exercise is to have students apply job analysis data and information in developing structured interview questions.

Instructions

- *Prior to class (optional):* You may want to print out a paper titled "Targeted Selection: A Behavioral Approach to Improving Hiring Decisions" (at http://www.ddiworld.com/resources/library/white-papers-monographs/targeted-selection-monograph) to share with students.
- Have students work on this brief exercise individually or in small groups.
- Inform students that their assignment is to develop three questions that could be used in a structured interview. Each question should address the following concerns:
  - To what job task does this question link?
  - What competencies/KSAOs are tapped by the question?
  - What are some examples of effective versus ineffective responses to this question?

- What could an interviewer ask as a follow-up question if the applicant does not initially provide sufficient information?
- Have individuals (or groups) present their questions to the class and ask for feedback.

Discussion Questions
- Was it easy to create these questions?
- If you have performed this job in the past, were you asked similar questions during your interview?
- Is it possible for a candidate to fake an interview? How might you address this problem?

Mock Interviews

Purpose The objective of this exercise is to have students experience what it is like both to undergo and to conduct a structured interview.

Instructions
- Create two versions of a structured interview with a few typical interview questions (e.g., "Tell me about a time you had to resolve a conflict," or "What would you do if a coworker took credit for your work?").
- Have students pair up and take turns role-playing interviewer and candidate. They should take brief notes when they are the interviewer so that they can report back to the rest of the class.
- Bring students back together to share examples of responses and impressions they had about the activity. It can be particularly helpful to illustrate how interviewers can use responses to understand what the applicant is like. For example, if a candidate talks about going to a boss to resolve a conflict rather than dealing with the person with whom he or she had the conflict, what might that say about how that person will function on the job?

Discussion Questions
- What was difficult about being the applicant?
- What could you do to prepare for an interview if you were an actual applicant?
- What was difficult about being the interviewer?
- What might you do as an interviewer to ensure you are being fair to all applicants? What might make that difficult?

How Predictors Are Selected in the Real World

Purpose By interviewing a supervisor, students will better understand the selection and use of predictors in real-world settings and be able to review this information in light of what they have learned in class.

Instructions

- This exercise works best as a written assignment.
- Have students identify a first-line supervisor or manager of any particular job (although the job they analyzed in the initial class assignment would be preferable). They should briefly interview the supervisor/manager face-to-face or over the phone.
- Interviews should address the following questions:
  - What is the typical selection process for this job?
  - Approximately how many candidates go through this process each month? Each year?
  - Do candidates fill out an application? If so, what does it look like?
  - Do you think your selection process has been successful in identifying good employees?
  - Is there anything you would change about the process? If so, what?
- Have students write up the results of their interview.
- You may want students to include answers to the discussion questions in their write-up if you do not have time to incorporate them into class discussion.

Discussion Questions

- Were you surprised at what you learned from the supervisor? If so, what was most surprising about the selection process?
- Is any part of the supervisor's selection process *not* in line with the methods described in class? If so, explain.
- How much does the real-world process differ from what you proposed in the earlier assignment (if "Identifying Predictors" was assigned)? Explain how the two processes are different and how they are the similar.

Faking on Personality Tests

Purpose The objective of this exercise is to have students engage in a simulated faking experiment, and use the results to talk about whether faking is an issue.

Instructions

- In class, provide students with two copies of a personality test (a few items from the International Personality Item Pool at http://ipip.ori.org/ is a good source). Ask students to take one honestly, and take another "faking good."
- Score the test (or if you are short on time, ask students to use a key to score their test), and show the averages to the class, pointing out what personality characteristics change for the "fake good" condition.
- Talk with students about the process of "faking good," using some of the discussion questions below to draw out some conversations about the experience.

Discussion Questions

- What did you change from your original answers to try to look better when you were faking good?
- Was it easy to fake good? What information did you draw on to help you judge how to change your answers?
- What might be some downsides to faking your answers to get a job? Are there potentially some benefits of hiring someone who is good at faking good?
- What do you think organizations could do to prevent or limit faking on these sorts of tests?

EVALUATING "TAKING IT TO THE FIELD"

The Chapter 6 activity involves a fireworks company that is asking for help with its selection battery. There are many possible critiques of and solutions to Pierce's problems. Below are some examples you might receive from your students.

Poor responses...	■ Fail to provide evidence for any assertions the student makes.
	■ Do not critique the current selection system or note only the most glaring problems.
	■ Do not provide any suggestions for improving the test battery or provide suggestions that will not improve prediction of performance or that are impractical (e.g., work sample, role-plays, assessment centers).
Good responses...	■ Note that the off-the-shelf application blank is problematic because it does not necessarily ask questions pertinent to the job and because some of the questions may be illegal.
	■ Note that the interview is unstructured, giving it less predictive power compared to structured interviews.
	■ Provide suggestions for assessing the applicant's ability to interact with customers, such as measures of extraversion, agreeableness, and emotional intelligence.
	■ Provide suggestions for identifying applicants with good attention to detail. Common suggestions may include conscientiousness tests, a work sample, or a test similar to the clerical test mentioned in the textbook. Cognitive ability tests may also be suggested; if so, students should explain how cognitive ability relates to detail orientation (e.g., those with higher cognitive ability are less prone to making mistakes).
	■ Provide suggestions for identifying individuals who are cool under pressure. Common suggestions might include tests of neuroticism, cognitive ability, or integrity.

Excellent responses...

- Note that the off-the-shelf application blank is problematic because it does not necessarily ask questions pertinent to the job and because some of the questions may be illegal.
- Note that the interview is unstructured, giving it less predictive power compared to structured interviews. Students may also note that the questions managers ask during these interviews could potentially be illegal. Students might also provide some examples of interview questions. Most students are not particularly skilled at writing interview questions without some specific direction, so you may see interview questions such as "Will you panic if something goes wrong?" Feedback on asking less obvious questions—such as "Tell me about a time you had to deal with an emergency"—will be helpful to those students.
- Provide suggestions for assessing the applicant's ability to interact with customers, such as measures of extraversion, agreeableness, and emotional intelligence.
- Provide suggestions for identifying applicants with good attention to detail. Common suggestions may include conscientiousness tests, a work sample, or a test similar to the clerical test mentioned in the textbook. Cognitive ability tests may also be suggested; if so, students should explain how cognitive ability relates to detail orientation (e.g., those with higher cognitive ability are less prone to mistakes).
- Provide suggestions for identifying individuals who are cool under pressure. Common suggestions might include tests of neuroticism, cognitive ability, or integrity.
- Indicate that the strength test does not do a good job of simulating the actual requirements for the job (e.g., at the shoot, there is no need to hold 80 pounds overhead; applicants just need to lift it out of a truck). Students should suggest establishing a strength test that better simulates the actual activities required on the job.

EVALUATING "APPLICATION QUESTIONS"

1. Many managers look for indications about how someone behaves outside of an interview and testing context. For example, if a candidate shows up late, is dressed in a sloppy way, or fails to send a thank-you note, the manager may no longer consider that person for the position. Do you think this is a valid predictor of performance? Should managers use information like this in making a hiring decision?

Evaluation Guide: Student responses to this question will likely vary. Common responses might include the following:

- Using something like lateness might screen out people who would actually be good at the job. For example, they could have been in an accident or encountered some other unavoidable delay. It would be unfair to penalize them for something out of their control.
- In some jobs, dressing professionally may not be relevant (e.g., people in tech support do not typically deal with clients and thus may not need to look as professional). However, how people are dressed may indicate how professional they are in other respects, which may be relevant.
- Make sure that students understand the difference between questions that prompt information about protected classes versus performance-relevant information. Also, indicate that all applicants should be judged equally, so if clothing for one applicant is considered relevant, it needs to be noted for all applicants. In addition, call students' attention to potential problems with judging aspects like grooming that might differ according to gender (e.g., expecting women to be more formally dressed than men for an interview) or race (e.g., deeming an Afro an unprofessional hairstyle, which would be discriminatory) as well as to other issues that could be problematic if used against a protected class.

2. There has been some recent debate about looking at job applicants' social media information (e.g., Facebook pages, Twitter accounts). Do you believe it is appropriate for managers to look at this type of information about a candidate? Why or why not? Do you think there might be any legal issues with looking at social media?

Evaluation Guide: Students will likely have some strong opinions. Some issues to note include the following:

- How an individual behaves on his or her personal pages may not represent how that person behaves in the workplace. Organizations should be careful not to discount strong candidates based on ambiguous information presented in these types of media.
- Organizations need to be cautious about viewing information about protected classes (e.g., marital status, age). Making decisions based on such information could lead to a lawsuit.
- Organizations need to treat all applicants equally, so they need to carefully look at these types of accounts if not all applicants have them.
- Students may benefit from a discussion about avoiding having inappropriate information or material on their Facebook pages and the like. For example, photos of people drinking or doing illicit drugs as well as negative posts about their organizations can prevent individuals from being hired or cause them to be fired. A discussion about ways to keep their professional and personal personas separate may be useful (e.g., using an altered name on their Facebook page so they are more difficult to find).

3. Imagine you are applying for a job and you know the company is looking for a candidate who is very conscientious and extraverted. Do you think the average person would be able to fake these traits on a personality test? How easy would it be for you, given that you have a little background in psychology? What might be some ways you could prevent or limit faking on these types of tests?

Evaluation Guide: This topic is controversial among I/O psychologists, so it might generate some interesting discussion among students. Here are some points worth making:

- Since students in this class are psychology students, they may have a better sense of what questions relate to what personality variables than do other people.
- If students believe they could fake traits on a test, ask whether they find it easy in most interviews to determine what types of answers managers are looking for—note that it is not always transparent what employers are looking for.
- This question also provides an opportunity to discuss different demographic variables that might lead to more or better faking/cheating (e.g., students with some training in psychology might have a better understanding of personality tests; highly conscientious people may be less likely to fake, and may believe others are less likely to fake).
- If students believe faking is easy, ask them whether this affects their opinion on whether these tests are effective for selection. Often, if students believe they can fake their way through tests, they also believe that other people can and will do so and thus think that organizations are making a poor choice by using personality tests.

4. Have you ever had a job that was described differently from what it actually turned out to be, or that had an aspect that surprised you when you started the job? What happened? What could the organization have done to better prepare you for the actual job?

Evaluation Guide: Students may have a variety of stories to share for this example. You might bring up the following points:

- In some cases, the organization might have unintentionally misrepresented a job—the position might have changed, or the person in charge of hiring might not have been aware of some of the minutiae of the job. In other cases, the organization might have intentionally misrepresented a job to get an applicant to join the organization. You might prompt students about the problems this could cause.
- Organizations could better prepare applicants for a job by, for example, preparing a good job analysis so as to describe the job accurately, giving applicants an opportunity to ask questions during their interviews, and allowing applicants or new hires to do some job shadowing.

5. Some workplaces conduct drug testing to ensure that their employees are not using recreational drugs. Do you agree with this practice? When might this practice be justified?

   Evaluation Guide: Student responses may vary. You could pose the following questions to generate discussion:
   - Is illegal drug use related to performance on a job? What about jobs where fine motor skills or mental clarity are important for keeping people safe?
   - Is it fair for organizations to judge employees on behaviors they engage in outside of work?
   - How might this affect employee attitudes about the workplace?

HIGHLIGHTED STUDY FOR DISCUSSION

Sachau, D., Congemi, P., Meyer, J., & Blackhurst, E. (n.d.). Should you hire BlazinWeedClown@Mail.com? Available at http://www.siop.org/tip/oct11/05sachau.aspx

Many articles on predictor measures are highly technical. If your students tend to be advanced, the recommended sources in the book are excellent for reviewing. However, for students with less experience with scholarly articles, this publication in *The I/O Psychologist* (TIP) is more accessible and might be better able to help them understand how researchers explore a potential predictor variable.

- In this study, the authors obtained applicant scores on personality and cognitive tests as well as e-mail names.
- The authors then coded e-mail names into three categories, with a number of subcategories: (1) inappropriate (e.g., armpitfart), (2) of questionable appropriateness (e.g., bballstud_23), and (3) appropriate (e.g., Jim.Johnson).
- Results indicated that individuals with inappropriate e-mail names scored lower on conscientiousness, professionalism, and work-related experience compared to those with appropriate names.
- One surprising finding was a lack of differences on cognitive ability. This would be a good opportunity for students to consider why someone who is very smart might have an inappropriate e-mail name. Students could also discuss whether there might be other problems with considering applicant e-mail names when making a hiring decision (e.g., would there be potential for discrimination unrelated to performance?).

WEB LEARNING

Title	Address
Online HR Guide: Personnel Selection	http://www.hr-guide.com/selection.htm
APA Information: Assessment Centers Help Companies Identify Future Managers	http://www.apa.org/research/action/managers.aspx
Assessment and Development Centre Design	http://www.psychometrics.co.uk/adc.htm
Hogan Personality Inventory	http://www.hoganassessments.com/hogan-personality-inventory
Society for Industrial and Organizational Psychology (SIOP): Types of Employment Tests	http://www.siop.org/Workplace/employment%20testing/testtypes.aspx
U.S. Office of Personnel Management: Assessment and Selection	http://www.opm.gov/policy-data-oversight/assessment-and-selection/
International Personnel Assessment Council (IPAC)	http://www.ipacweb.org
Information on the Five-Factor Model of Personality	http://www.personalityresearch.org/bigfive.html
The Personality Project	http://www.personality-project.org
Developmental Dimensions International (DDI)	http://www.ddiworld.com

Selection Decisions and Personnel Law

Chapter Summary

Whereas Chapter 6 discussed the many types of predictors used in employee selection, this chapter presented information about how to use those predictors in making selection decisions. Predictive validation, concurrent validation, validity generalization, and synthetic validation were examined in light of how important they are for employee selection. Recruitment was also discussed as an important precursor to employee selection, and the recent role of social media in this process was examined.

Various approaches to the selection process were discussed, including the multiple cutoff, multiple hurdle, and multiple regression techniques. This part of the discussion provided both a how-to guide and an overview of the differences among these approaches. A lengthy discussion of utility followed; here we noted that if a selection battery is not viewed as useful for an organization, the organization is unlikely to be interested in it. We also looked at two ways in which decision accuracy can be operationalized: decision accuracy for hires and overall decision accuracy. Validity, base rate, selection ratio, and cost were identified as important factors affecting the utility of a new selection battery.

The last half of the chapter was spent on legal issues in industrial psychology. The emphasis was on selection, as it is in this area that legal issues tend to emerge most often. First, we discussed the history of the EEOC. Next, we examined employment at-will, adverse impact, and affirmative action, as these are among the most important concepts one must understand in order to appreciate the context and procedures involved in personnel law. Finally, we considered the major employment laws currently in place (see Table 7.8). Distinctions were drawn between disparate treatment and disparate impact, between *quid pro quo* harassment and hostile work environment harassment, between BFOQ defenses and job-relatedness defenses, and between reasonable accommodation and undue hardship.

TEACHING THE CHAPTER

There are three interrelated topics presented in this chapter: recruitment, selection decisions, and employment law. The recruitment portion of the chapter presents an opportunity to stimulate class conversation about what types of things attract people to apply for a job in an organization. Do they look at how nice the recruitment material appears, do they focus on certain types of information, or do they simply look for a name brand that they recognize? The dramatic increase in the role of the Internet in recruitment efforts also takes center stage in this chapter and is worth discussing with students. Who is the primary audience for online recruiting efforts? What are the legal implications of using the Internet to recruit and attract employees?

The second part of the chapter is dedicated to a discussion of selection decisions. Specifically, validation and regression approaches to selection are discussed—though they should be a review of information presented in Chapter 2. However, this chapter further offers students the opportunity to integrate that material into the practical application of making a selection decision. In addition, the second exercise presented below is designed to allow you to demonstrate the complexity of selection decisions as well as how decisions may differ depending on predictor weighting and how cutoffs are used. Discussion around the value of I/O and HR in organizations may result from the chapter's coverage of utility.

The chapter concludes with a primer on employment law, which is important to organizations, I/O psychology, and society as a whole. Personnel laws have been established, and currently are used, to help level the organizational playing field for groups that have historically experienced discrimination in employment and society. Laws are also designed to give certain protections from overzealous corporate interests. Therefore, students are likely to be very engaged in discussing the legal implications of employment decisions even if they do not plan to become an employment litigator. One of the exercises below was developed to help students gain exposure to employment law and legal research. Mainstream media outlets, such as major newspapers and magazines, also may be fruitful sources of legal issues pertaining to employment decisions. You may want to consider integrating such current articles into your classroom discussions to give students a glimpse of how these laws affect employees and organizations in real time.

SUGGESTED EXERCISES AND ASSIGNMENTS

The Internet and Recruitment

Purpose The main objective of this exercise is to examine a variety of employers' websites and determine the factors that make the employers and their respective websites attractive to potential applicants.

Instructions

- Have students identify a job and an industry they are interested in researching. This may be the job/industry for which they conducted their earlier job analysis in Chapter 3.
- Ask students to go to a major Internet job board (e.g., monster.com, hotjobs.com, or careerbuilder.com) and enter their target job.
- Ask students to identify as few as two or three companies (or as many as eight to ten) that have posted jobs on the job board. They should use the links to the employers' websites to examine the employers' recruitment pages. Have students report (in written or presentation format) on the characteristics of these sites, guided by the following questions:
  - What are the major differences and similarities between the sites?
  - Can you tell by the website's presentation what target audience the company is trying to attract?
  - What kind of information is presented on each site (e.g., salary ranges, workplace diversity, realistic job previews)?
  - What aesthetic aspects of the websites are attractive to you (e.g., animation, pictures, interactivity)?
  - To what extent is it easy to get information about the job from the website? Does it seem easy to contact someone at the organization?
  - Can an applicant apply online?

Discussion Questions

- What stood out as the major similarities and differences across these websites?
- Were there any sites that definitely would have/would not have led you to apply for a job?
- Aside from using the employers' recruitment web pages, how else might job applicants use the Internet in their job search?
- How might employers use the Internet to learn more about potential applicants (e.g., Facebook, LinkedIn, etc.)?

Reality Show and Selection

Purpose The main objective of this exercise is to engage students by providing an example of an unusual approach to selection, and encourage them to devise their own approach. This activity can work in a single class period, but also makes a good group project that can extend over several class periods.

Instructions

- There are a number of interesting reality shows on TV that make contestants compete for a job or opportunity. Examples of this might include *America's Next Top Model* (for a supermodel job), *Face Off* (for a job working as a special effects makeup artist, *Food Network Star* (to become a cooking show personality), and *Inkmasters* (for a tattoo artist job). Have students watch an episode of the show, or watch some excerpts in class.
- Next, have students work in groups to devise a reality show competition for a job—interesting and creative jobs might be particularly fun (e.g., astronaut, spy, surfing instructor). What challenges might they set up for contestants that would showcase their skills? Who should judge these activities? How?
- Ask students to present their competition show to the class. Encourage other students to come up with other ideas to ensure that the winner of the competition would actually be good at the job.

Discussion Questions

- Do the challenges on these shows do a good job of testing contestants' skills? Why or why not?
- Have the contestants on these shows actually demonstrated success after the show? What might this say about the validity of this approach to selection?
- What might be a problem with using something like this for selection? What might affect its validity, as well as the type of people who would be attracted to this type of competition?

Making Selection Decisions for a Bookstore

Purpose This exercise will give students experience in applying the principles learned in the chapter regarding selection decisions (multiple scores, multiple cutoffs, multiple regression) to a practical example.

Instructions

- *Prior to class:* Copy the table below into a format you can present to students during class (reproduce in an electronic file if a virtual classroom is used, or on your classroom board). You will not reveal the entire table at first.
- Begin by informing students that you will be staffing a bookstore with one manager, three sales clerks, and two warehouse workers.
- Next, show students the first row of the table, which illustrates all of the various predictors to be used. Ask the class which two predictors in the table they

would use to make a selection decision for hiring a bookstore manager. Then have the class calculate scores to demonstrate who should be chosen for the job.

- Ask students what they feel is absolutely necessary to perform the manager job and create a cutoff score (note that all scores range from 1 to 10).
- Then have students run through a variety of scenarios for hiring sales clerks and warehouse workers. Have the class note how the different equations and combinations of cutoff scores change the composition of who should be hired for which job.
- Feel free to use the information in the table in as many different ways as you would like, depending on what issue and element you would like to highlight.

Discussion Questions
- What is your impression of the challenges facing organizations when making selection decisions?
- Would you implement a multiple hurdle approach for any of the three jobs? Why or why not?

Table for use with this exercise:									
Applicant	Gender	Big 5	Exp.	Intrvw.	Sit. Judgment	Cog. Abil.	Total	Regression Equation$_1$	Regression Equation$_2$
Donald	M	Hi E, Lo C	8	8	6	7	29	19.96	23.40
Terry	F	Hi A, Lo C	1	7	4	4	16	7.44	20.44
Brian	M	Lo E, Hi C	6	8	10	7	31	18	23.44
April	F	Hi N, Hi C	4	6	4	10	24	14.04	18.62
Peter	M	Hi E, Lo C	2	2	1	4	9	6.67	7.52
Anita	F	Hi E, Lo C	5	10	8	7	30	16.58	25.88
Jim	M	Lo E, Hi C	3	7	3	8	21	11.78	18.79
Diane	F	Lo O, Hi A	2	9	7	3	21	9.92	20.79
Cut Scores									
Manager		Hi E	4	7	5	4	20	12.20	18.21
Sales		Hi A	3	6	4	4	17	10.14	15.72
Inventory		Hi C	2	2	1	4	9	6.67	7.52

Regression Equation$_1$ = 1.2 + 1.5 (Experience) + .3 (Interview) + .26 (Sit. Judgment) + .4 (Cog. Abil.)
Regression Equation$_2$ = 1.2 + .5 (Experience) + 1.73 (Interview) + .26 (Sit. Judgment) + .4 (Cog. Abil.)

Gratz v. Bollinger Case

Purpose This exercise will provide students with an example of a case that had an important impact on selection of students at Michigan State.

Instructions

- Introduce the *Gratz v. Bollinger* case. There are several videos available of the case; for example, *Tom Brokaw Reports: Affirmative Action Hour* provides a good overview of the case. Alternatively, you can provide a handout with the details of the case.
- After the case has been presented, you could take an anonymous poll to see where students stand on the case (or on affirmative action in general) or divide the class in half and ask them to argue one side versus the other.
- Debrief by talking about any updates to selection law that have occurred since the video; indicate to students that the laws change frequently, so it can sometimes be difficult to navigate selection unless one is up-to-date on cases.

Discussion Questions

- Do you believe that there will ever truly be equality between races in the United States?
- What do you think it means to be "fair"?
- What are some arguments for affirmative action? Against affirmative action?
- Is diversity important for the workplace? Why or why not?

What Is Reasonable?

Purpose The point of this exercise is to help students think about some of the intricacies involved in determining what changes to an organization or job seem reasonable to accommodate an employee with a disability.

Instructions

- Pair up students. Ask students to consider an employment position they have had in the past or one that they are relatively familiar with in terms of its core tasks. Ask them to think of a disability someone might have (e.g., hearing impairment, visual impairment, mobility issues).
- Have the pairs discuss which of the position's tasks might be difficult for someone with this disability to perform. How difficult would it be for the organization to change the job to accommodate this disability? What tools and technology might help to accommodate a disabled employee?
- Have the pairs share with the class some key points of their discussion.

Discussion Questions

- What are some examples of changes you believe are reasonable? Which changes seem like they might cause an organization undue hardship?
- Why is it important for organizations to accommodate people with disabilities?

- What steps can organizations take to be proactive about welcoming people with disabilities into the workforce?

Employment Law

Purpose The objective of this exercise is to give students exposure to the many legal decisions involving employment issues.

Instructions

You should conduct this exercise after lecturing about the major employment laws. This exercise is best suited for a classroom that includes computer technology for all students. However, if you do not have this type of classroom, you may want to identify a particular case or cases in advance for students to review and discuss.

- Divide students into small groups.
- Assign each group to one of the major employment laws discussed in class: the Civil Rights Act (1964, 1991), Equal Pay Act, Americans with Disabilities Act (ADA), Age Discrimination in Employment Act (ADEA), or Family and Medical Leave Act (FMLA).
- Provide students with the following Internet resources for this exercise:
  - http://www.hr-guide.com
  - http://www.supremecourtus.gov
  - http://www.dol.gov/elaws
- Have each group report the following to the rest of the class:
  - A brief overview of the law (this should be a review, since it was already discussed in class)
  - A general statement of why the law is important to organizations and employees
  - An example of a case that is based on that law, including the following information:
    - Who were the parties involved? Plaintiff(s)? Defendant(s)?
    - What was the key issue brought by the plaintiff(s)?
    - What was the final outcome (i.e., the legal decision)?
    - What was the implication of this case for upholding the law?
- As can be seen, this is a very involved exercise, which may take close to an entire class period. Alternatively, you may want to identify one of the primary laws and a relevant case in advance. Also, at the time of teaching this class, there may be an important case being reviewed in the court system that will serve as an effective example.

Discussion Questions

- In the case that you reviewed, what did the judges rely on most when making their decision?
- As an I/O psychologist or HR manager, how would you stay current on court decisions affecting employment laws?

EVALUATING "TAKING IT TO THE FIELD"

This activity asks students to do a number of things. First, it asks them to indicate whether adverse impact is occurring at John Marshall's pork-processing plants. Second, it asks them to consider whether the company's current selection processes are legal and, if not, what needs to be done to make them legal. Student responses may vary, but guidelines for responses are below:

Adverse Impact Calculations*			
Comparison	Majority Group Ratio	Minority Group Ratio	Adverse Impact Calculation
African American and Caucasian American	300/400 = .75	120/200 = .60	.80
Latino American and Caucasian American	400/500 = .80	120/200 = .60	.75
Latino American and African American	400/500 = .80	300/400 = .75	.94

*Because there are no Asian Americans applying for the job, we are unable to calculate a ratio for that group.

Poor responses…	▪ Provide only a blanket response (e.g., "Yes, it is legal") without explaining how they have come to that conclusion. ▪ Fail to provide any information *or* calculations on adverse impact *or* provide incorrect calculations for adverse impact. ▪ Do not critically evaluate each selection component *or* provide only very general critiques that will not be useful to the client.
Good responses…	▪ Provide correct (or mostly correct) adverse impact calculations and indicate that there is adverse impact when comparing the Caucasian Americans and Latino Americans (with the Latino Americans as the majority group). ▪ Should note that the neuroticism test is legal because it measures performance and is not likely to be different among the racial groups. ▪ Should note that the strength test is potentially one test that is causing the differences among the hiring rates for each race. Students should note that adverse impact is not automatically illegal, and they can make one of two arguments: ▪ Because hand strength is job-relevant, as indicated by the validation evidence, this qualification is a BFOQ and is therefore legal despite the adverse impact it causes.

- The organization can make reasonable accommodations so that the hand strength requirement is loosened.
- With respect to the work experience component, note that this is another likely source of the adverse impact. Students should indicate that there is no validity evidence for this component, so it is not clear whether this predictor is actually related to job performance.

Excellent responses...

- Provide correct adverse impact calculations, and indicate that there is adverse impact when comparing the Caucasian Americans and Latino Americans (with the Latino Americans as the majority group). Students may also mention that because the African American and Caucasian American comparison is right at the .80 cutoff, the organization may want to consider implementing an affirmative action program to head off any potential problems.
- Indicate that whichever group has the highest hiring rate is considered the majority in a selection context, even if it is a race that is typically referred to as a minority (e.g., Latinos).
- Note that because no Asian Americans applied, there is no way to calculate an adverse impact ratio for that group. Students could mention that the organization may want to consider initiating an Affirmative Action Plan to get some qualified Asian American applicants into the hiring process.
- Note that the neuroticism test is legal because it measures performance and is not likely to be different among the racial groups.
- Note that the strength test is potentially causing the differences among the hiring rates for each race. Students should note that adverse impact is not automatically illegal, and they can make one of two arguments:
  - Because hand strength is job-relevant, as indicated by the validation evidence, this qualification is a BFOQ and is therefore legal despite the adverse impact it causes.
  - The organization can make reasonable accommodations so that the hand strength requirement is loosened. Students may suggest that the jobs could be rearranged so that hand strength is not integral to some positions or that workers could work to improve their hand strength after they have been hired.
  - With respect to the work experience component, note that this is another likely source of the adverse impact. Students should indicate that there is no validity evidence for this component, so it is not clear whether this predictor is actually related to job performance. Students should suggest implementing a validity study to evaluate whether experience predicts performance.

EVALUATING "APPLICATION QUESTIONS"

1. This chapter mentions person–environment fit. When you are looking for a job, what are some cues that indicate an organization is a "good fit" for you? Have you ever been in an organization that wasn't a good fit for you? What happened?

   Evaluation Guide: Students will likely have good stories about organizations that did not fit them. Some points to make during the discussion:
   - Fit is subjective; for one person, a very casual work environment may be enjoyable, while other people prefer more professional environments.
   - When people don't fit in, there are a number of consequences. First, people may find that they are unable to assimilate well—they may not be invited out to socialize, other workers may avoid them, or they may end up feeling lonely and unsupported. Second, people are much more likely to quit when they don't fit in.
   - Students may have some good ideas for helping people to feel that they fit in—for example, making sure that everyone is introduced to a coworker or praising and supporting coworkers will often help them feel more accepted by their peers, even if they don't see eye to eye on some issues in the workplace.

2. In some states, the medicinal use of marijuana is allowed to treat certain conditions, such as glaucoma and anxiety. In these states, do you think it would be legal to require applicants to take a drug test? What might be some problems with implementing this requirement? If an organization wants to use a drug test, what steps might you suggest they follow?

   Evaluation Guide: As of the writing of this instructors' guide, case law on drug testing for medicinal marijuana is up in the air. However, this gives students a good opportunity to think about how drug legislation affects organizational practices. The following points are worth highlighting:
   - Note that organizations must be thoughtful about ADA requirements. If an individual has a condition that requires the use of marijuana to treat it, they may have a valid argument for being able to test positive for the drug.
   - Have students generate some reasons for why an organization can make an argument that marijuana use, legal or not, might relate to performance (e.g., higher absenteeism among users, lower work performance among users).
   - Have students generate some problems that may be created by requiring employees to abstain from marijuana—how might these employees feel about the organization telling them what they can and cannot do in their free time, or with their medical treatment? How much does the legality of the drug matter in these perceptions (e.g., would employees be comfortable with an organization telling them they could not use cocaine? That they could not use alcohol?)

- Encourage students to walk through the process they would use to determine whether any other requirement is legal. Does it cause adverse impact? Is it a BFOQ or a job requirement? What types of jobs might we be able to make a good argument for a drug-free workplace (e.g., construction worker, driver, or similar risky occupations)?
- Note to students that it can be important to make policies clear and fair for employees. Changing a drug-testing policy requires updating employee handbooks and educating current employees about the policy.

3. How common are BFOQs? Interview five people about their jobs and determine whether someone in a protected class (race, color, religion, national origin, sex, age, disability) would be unable to perform an essential job function.

Evaluation Guide: Students may have a variety of interesting examples. Issues related to disability tend to be most evident to students, as many of them have been engaged in types of manual labor (e.g., roofing or housepainting). However, encourage students to also think about what types of jobs might require characteristics that could be related to protected classes, such as the following:

- Janitors, dressing room attendants, or security officers may need to be a certain gender in order to perform their duties (e.g., patting down a female offender).
- Some jobs may have a height requirement. Women and some racial/ethnic groups may tend to be shorter, which can lead to discrimination based on a BFOQ.
- Jobs in religious institutions can sometimes be exempt from many of these requirements. Currently, religious institutions are allowed to refuse to hire people who are of a different religion. Recent cases have also supported religious institutions in not hiring people with disabilities if it is deemed that they are unable to complete aspects of their job because of it.

4. Consider a job you have had. Provide one example of a reasonable accommodation that could be made so an applicant with a disability could do the job. What types of changes do you believe would be unreasonable (i.e., cause undue hardship for the company)?

Evaluation Guide: It is important to emphasize that what is considered reasonable is fairly complex, and lawyers and other experts would likely be consulted. However, it is a good thought experiment to have students balance the needs of the employee against the needs of the organization. Some potential accommodations that students may discuss include the following:

- Putting in ramps (which is likely reasonable).
- Putting in an elevator (unlikely to be reasonable for some organizations).
- Putting up Braille signs (likely to be reasonable).
- Changing a job so that a small component is completed by someone else. For example, if filing is part of the job and someone in a wheelchair is unable to access some of the drawers, this would likely be reasonable. However, if a job requires this behavior quite a bit, it may be deemed unreasonable to completely change the job to accommodate a person who is disabled.

5. Typically races other than Caucasians are considered to be minorities. Are there any jobs where one might expect a different racial group to be hired more often than Caucasians? In these cases, would you recommend that the organization enact an AAP? Why or why not?

Evaluation Guide: This may be a rather controversial question for some students. Some issues to consider:

- In I/O psychology, "minority" is typically discussed in terms of the number of people who are least selected. So in some positions, Caucasians may be considered a minority. Be aware, however, than many other approaches to racial differences define "minority" less by numbers and more by privileges or social status. Explaining that different philosophies and approaches exist will be helpful to students.

- In the United States, there have been instances of Caucasian individuals successfully suing an organization that selects a higher proportion of other races (what is sometimes referred to as "reverse discrimination"), so organizations need to be aware of this possibility.

- If students come up with jobs that tend to be highly populated by minority members (e.g., in the food industry and in manufacturing), it may be helpful to talk about why that is the case (e.g., different access to education and jobs for different groups of people).

- Students are likely to have many opinions on whether an AAP is appropriate. This is an important point for gauging whether students understand key concepts from the chapter, including that AAPs are not quota systems and there are a variety of noncontroversial ways to enact them, that AAPs should not result in unqualified workers being hired, and that sometimes AAPs can have important effects on how hired minorities are viewed in the organization.

- As an additional illustration, you might consider discussing gender, and whether it is easier to get men into female-dominated fields (e.g., nursing) versus women into male-dominated fields (e.g., firefighters). What problems crop up in these cases, and what are some benefits of greater diversity in these jobs?

6. In the United States, new mothers are given 12 weeks of unpaid leave. Some countries provide paid maternity leave (e.g., Portugal), paternity leave (e.g., Sweden), or longer periods of unpaid leave (e.g., Japan). What are some advantages and disadvantages of the U.S. policy? What changes (if any) would you make to the U.S. policy?

Evaluation Guide: Many students are unaware of some of the policies in other countries, including forced maternity/paternity leave, longer leaves, and paid leave. You may want to indicate the following points:

- The United States tends to have a longer workweek and less vacation time than other countries. As a result, the United States tends to be quite productive and rich as a country.

- In countries (such as Germany) where women are given a great deal of leave, it can sometimes be difficult to convince companies to hire women because of the risk of losing them. If protection is not offered for this type of discrimination, it can be difficult for women to obtain work.
- In terms of disadvantages, U.S. women may be discouraged from working or from having both children and a career. In addition, it can be difficult for women to obtain prestigious positions in the organization. You may wish to discuss with students what women can offer in the workplace and why it might be problematic to discourage them from moving up.
- You can also note that 12 weeks of unpaid maternity leave is what is legally required, but organizations can also implement their own policies that are more generous. You could ask students what organizations can do to help working mothers (e.g., implementing paternal leave, providing lactation rooms, helping women reenter the workforce after their leave).

HIGHLIGHTED STUDY FOR DISCUSSION

Resendez, M. G. (2002). The stigmatizing effects of affirmative action: An examination of moderating variables. *Journal of Applied Social Psychology, 32,* 185–206.

This article is a two-part study exploring the effects of stigma on minorities in affirmative action (AA) hiring situations. For the most part, the article is short and accessible, but it may be helpful to point out to students that the variables are coded in a way that may not be intuitive (higher scores indicate more negative attitudes). Main points of the article include the following:

- Study 1 was a 2×3 factorial design, where qualification (high versus moderate) and race (Black, White, and affirmative action Black) were manipulated in a hiring scenario. Participants rated competence, projected career progress, hiring as a result of qualifications, activity, potency, perceived early deprivation, and perceived difficulty in obtaining employment.
- Results indicated that qualified applicants were seen as more competent, had better projected career success, were more likely to be hired due to qualifications, were more active, were less potent, and faced fewer obstacles.
- In terms of race, affirmative action hires were seen as less competent (compared to both Black and White applicants), were less likely to be hired due to qualifications (compared to both Black and White applicants), and faced more obstacles (compared to Black applicants).
- The second study manipulated qualifications (superior versus equal to another candidate) and race/status (White, Hispanic, Hispanic hire with elimination of discrimination Affirmative Action Plan (AAP), and Hispanic hire with preferential treatment AAP).
- Participants read scenarios and rated the hiree on how well they thought the hiree would do compared to other employees, on the hiree's projected career progress, and on the fairness of the hiring procedure.

- Results indicated that Hispanics on AAPs were rated as less competent than both Hispanics without an AAP and White hires. Hispanic hires in both AAP conditions were also expected to experience less career progress than Hispanics without an AAP and Whites. Finally, Hispanics in both AAP conditions were believed to have been hired for reasons other than their qualifications.

- Results also indicated that participants' attitudes toward AAPs affected their judgments of hires. Specifically, participants who believed AAPs were unfair were more likely to feel negatively about an AAP hire's competence, career progress, and hiring based on qualifications. Students may have a number of interesting opinions about this finding.

- The authors indicate that applicants who are hired under AAPs experience a sense of stigma, even when their qualifications are superior to those of other applicants. The authors suggest that, rather than eliminating AAPs, the public should be better informed about them. They also suggest that more education about institutional discrimination may prevent this stigma from forming. These opinions may provide a segue for fruitful discussion about I/O psychologists' role in educating the public about AA and AAPs so that AAP hires can be more effective in the workplace.

WEB LEARNING

Title	Address
HR Guide: Personnel Selection	http://www.hr-guide.com/selection.htm
HR Recruitment: Toolbox for the HR Community	http://recruiting.hr.toolbox.com/groups/?reftrk=no&cid=39924779
Workforce Management website	http://www.workforce.com
StatSoft.com: Multiple Regression	http://www.statsoft.com/textbook/stmulreg.html
Business Management Daily HR Resources	http://www.businessmanagementdaily.com/human-resources#_
Employment Law Watch	http://www.employmentlawwatch.com
Americans with Disabilities Act (ADA) website	http://www.ada.gov
U.S. Supreme Court: Recent Opinions	http://www.supremecourt.gov/opinions/opinions.aspx
U.S. Equal Employment Opportunity Commission (EEOC)	http://www.eeoc.gov
Employment Law Information Network	http://www.elinfonet.com

Training and Development

This chapter should help students understand:

- How important training is to both organizations and employees
- How to diagnose an organization's training needs through the use of organizational, task, person, and demographic analyses
- The basic principles of learning that affect training success, such as meaningfulness, practice, overlearning, and feedback
- What makes an organization's learning context conducive to successful training
- Each of the various training techniques, as well as their strengths and weaknesses
- The key elements of transfer of training
- The traditional criteria used in training evaluation, along with a newer perspective on these criteria
- How to design a training evaluation study in a number of different ways
- The increasing importance and prevalence of both sexual harassment training and diversity training

Chapter Summary

This chapter was structured around five major areas. First, we discussed how organizations are diagnosed with respect to training needs. The organizational analysis identifies where training is needed in the organization, the task analysis identifies which behaviors or duties have to be improved through training, and the person analysis identifies those employees who need to be trained. In addition, demographic analysis may indicate the training needs of particular employee populations.

Second, the learning context and its role in training effectiveness were considered. Some learning principles were defined and then applied to specific training issues. As discussed, these principles can play a critical role in the success of a training program. For instance, we noted that trainees may fail to learn effectively if the material to be learned is too extensive and cumbersome; if the material is not meaningful; if practice is rarely used or done poorly; if the desired behaviors are not overlearned; and if immediate, specific feedback is not provided. We also discovered that the transfer of learned behaviors and skills back to the workplace is contingent on many factors that make up the learning context.

Third, we discussed training delivery methods, with an emphasis on the role technology has played in the development of new and varied approaches. Many of the most frequently used specific techniques were discussed, along with examples and empirical evidence.

Fourth, we examined the evaluation of training programs. We discussed Kirkpatrick's four levels of criteria (reaction, learning, behavioral, results), as well as the augmented framework presented by Alliger and his colleagues. In addition, we discussed a few commonly used training evaluation designs.

Finally, we spent some time considering a recent trend in the training literature—diversity. In particular, we discussed issues related to both sexual harassment training and general workplace diversity training, with a consideration of the role these play in today's organizations and an examination of effectiveness where possible.

TEACHING THE CHAPTER

Training, one of the more dynamic topics in I/O psychology, is covered in Chapter 8. An ironic aspect of covering this topic is that you will be discussing training in one of the most common training environments—the classroom. There are many options you can use to make this material interesting and bring it to life for your students. In addition, to complement your lecture, students are likely to have experience participating in some form of job training and will be able to share stories about their experiences. In fact, one of the exercises below capitalizes on students' personal experiences with job training to help reinforce the material about training evaluation.

In addition to the exercises provided below, there are numerous training websites on the Internet. These can be used during class to help students gain practical insight into the fundamentals of training (see links below). Also, the increasing use of, popularity of, and generally positive reactions to multimedia/video training presentations are discussed in this chapter. Hundreds of training videos are available, and you may find that companies will provide you with demo copies for educational purposes. One website that may be particularly useful is http://www.trainingabc.com/john-cleese -training-videos-DVDs/ which demonstrates and sells training videos. The Video Arts series featuring *Monty Python's* John Cleese is sure to be entertaining for any class.

Finally, you can stimulate class discussion by holding a debate about a very fast-growing training phenomenon—online training. Many Fortune 500 companies as well as many universities and colleges are using online training techniques. In fact, entire universities are now located only on the Internet. You may want to focus a debate on the pros and cons of online training (from the both the trainees' and the organization's perspective), the potential ethical issues regarding online training, whether online training is more efficient for student or employee learning, and who benefits most from this training format.

SUGGESTED EXERCISES AND ASSIGNMENTS

Using Job Analysis Data to Inform Training Needs Analysis

Purpose Students will examine and apply their job analysis data to devise a training needs assessment.

Instructions

- *Prior to class:* Give this assignment to students prior to class, then discuss it at the beginning of the class period after the assignment is turned in.
- This assignment involves conducting a training needs assessment for the job they analyzed earlier in the course.
- Students' assignments should include the following sections:
  - *Brief summary of job analysis:* Include a list of tasks that are performed on the job, the KSAOs that are necessary for successful performance, and the current training that an employee in that position must complete.
  - *Identify and distinguish KSAOs:* Identify which KSAOs are needed for an employee to be selected, which must be performed on the first day of the job, and which can be taught once a person is hired by the organization.
  - *Recommend which KSAOs and tasks should be the focus of training* in order for the employee to be deemed competent in the current job.
  - *Recommend training* that can be provided to prepare employees for long-term success in the company.

Discussion Questions

- Do you think that employees for your job receive adequate training based on what you learned during your job analysis and your overall experience with people in this job?
- Was it difficult to distinguish the KSAOs needed on the first day from the ones that could be taught?

Designing a Training Program

Purpose Students will consider and practice designing a training program.

Instructions

- Divide students into groups of four to six.
- Have students design a training program for one of the following activities (you may need to provide a larger number of activities depending on your class size):
  - Throwing a party
  - Cleaning an apartment
  - Studying for a test
  - Going grocery shopping
  - Taking the SAT

- ■ Giving a speech
- ■ Grooming a dog
- ■ Cooking a meal
■ Have each group identify critical behaviors/tasks that lead to effective performance, explain how those behaviors/tasks will be taught, specify why they will be using the methods they selected, and provide a clear description of criteria for successful performance.
■ Give groups 15 to 25 minutes to design their training programs. Then, for the remainder of the class period, have groups share their training programs with the other students.

Discussion Questions

■ Did your group encounter any difficulties agreeing on criteria for successful performance?
■ How would you measure whether your training program was a success?
■ Will the training program you designed help you perform the task better than before? Why or why not?

Instructional Designer/Trainer for the Day

Purpose In this exercise, students will apply their new knowledge about learning principles and consider ways to effectively train an employee given practical considerations.

Instructions

■ Divide students into groups of four to six.
■ Have groups design the curriculum for a one-day training session for entry-level retail salespeople. If you would like the formal description of tasks and KSAOs necessary for this job, visit O★NET Online, job code #41.2031.00, at http://online.onetcenter.org/link/summary/41-2031.00.
■ The following parameters should guide this assignment:
  ■ Trainees have limited job experience and will begin working in a retail store tomorrow, which is the first day of the holiday shopping season.
  ■ Your store has a strong reputation within its industry for excellent customer service and low prices. Salespeople do not receive commission on sales, and the work environment is characterized as highly collaborative and cooperative.
  ■ The following tasks and KSAOs must be addressed during a training session that will last approximately eight hours (9:00 A.M. to 5:00 P.M.):
    ■ Customer service
    ■ Cash register operation
    ■ Organizational culture
    ■ Inventory management
  ■ For each component of training, have groups explain why they chose a specific methodology to train the employees. Also, instruct them to clearly link the training components to the KSAOs/tasks that are necessary for successful performance on the job.

- The trainees are likely to be between the ages of 18 and 25, and it is crucial to keep them engaged. Tell students that the company wants them to be creative and consider things like multimedia videos, simulations, and so on.
- Tell students that the product of their work should look like a schedule or agenda for the training day. It should include a timeline, a description of the training activities, and explanations of why they chose the activities/methods they did.

Discussion Questions

- Do you feel like you could accomplish all of the required tasks/KSAOs in the time you have for training? Do you think one day is enough time to prepare the person for the job?
- Have you ever attended a similar training? What was the experience like? What made the training interesting (or not interesting)?
- How would you gauge trainees' reactions to this training?

Organizational Socialization

Purpose The objective of this exercise is to discuss the importance of, and informal methods for, organizational socialization.

Instructions

- This exercise can be conducted as a class discussion or in groups.
- Ask students to discuss examples of instances when they felt they were socialized into an organization (it can be a work organization or a social organization). Specifically, how did they obtain the information (attitudes, behaviors, knowledge) that they needed to be an organizational member?
- The discussion should focus on the informal techniques they used, not necessarily on formal training programs.

Discussion Questions

- Facilitate students' reactions and responses to their experience with socialization. Did students feel they were adequately socialized into their organization's culture? Was socialization necessary to perform the job or role? How did the socialization process affect their view of the organization?
- Is there a socialization process that happens upon entering college? If so, how does it happen and how does it differ from the socialization process an employee might experience?

The Value of Active Learning

Purpose This exercise will provide students with a simple illustration of the importance of active learning and practice in training.

Instructions

- Devise a moderately complex task to teach students. For example, you might teach them how to make an origami crane or how to execute a magic trick.

Whatever you choose, be certain it requires some physical movement and several steps that must be done in succession.

- Divide the class into two groups. One group should receive the materials you use so they can follow along step-by-step; the other group should not receive the materials.
  - If you have a larger class, you could add a third condition, such as a group that hears the instructions several times before attempting to replicate the task or a group that takes notes on the task.
- After you are done teaching the students how to complete the task, give them an opportunity to replicate it.
- If some students struggle with the task, have students who were successful help their classmates.

Discussion Questions

- Which group appeared to have the most success in completing the task? Why?
- How does this translate to the workplace? What steps can we take to help trainees be actively engaged in what they are learning?
- How can you also apply this to school? What steps can you take to be engaged in classes and to actively learn material?

Evaluating the Effectiveness of Training

Purpose The objective of this exercise is to have students apply their own work experiences to learn about the application of training criteria in practice.

Instructions

- Divide students into groups of four to six.
- Have groups design a training evaluation form to assess the training experienced by one of the group members. Thus, one of the group members needs to describe an employee training experience. Based on this experience, groups should create an evaluation form that is one page in length.
- Items/methods included in the evaluation should measure the following training criteria:
  - Affective reactions
  - Utility reactions
  - Immediate posttraining learning
  - Behavioral demonstration
- Groups should also describe how the long-term effectiveness of the training would be evaluated and what could be done to reinforce the training going forward.

Discussion Questions

- How effective was the assessment of the actual training experienced by the person in the group? Was there any attempt to evaluate training at the time it took place, or did the evaluation come later?

- What do most training evaluations seem to measure? Do these seem to be useful constructs/criteria?
- Why do you think organizations might not follow up on training?

EVALUATING "TAKING IT TO THE FIELD"

For the Chapter 8 activity, a Florida bar is requesting help designing a training program for servers that is quick, cheap, and effective. The owner also asks for help determining how to address problems with training transfer and behaviors. A general guide to responses is provided below.

Poor responses…	■ Provide feedback that is too vague to be helpful (e.g., "You need to do a better job of training servers").
	■ Propose large changes to the job itself (e.g., "Servers shouldn't be required to enter their own orders into the cash register").
	■ Provide suggestions that are impractical or go against what Imani has requested (e.g., day-long training programs, comments about Imani's leadership ability).
Good responses…	■ Suggest that Imani more carefully select which servers the new hires shadow. Some servers may be teaching a number of bad habits to new employees, which could be part of the problem.
	■ Identify different ways that Imani could organize and deliver the training. Most of the suggested techniques should rely on empirically supported techniques, such as distributed practice or active learning.
	■ Should identify opportunities for servers to receive timely and relevant feedback on their performance; for example, having the trainer shadow the new server.
	■ Should avoid the use of expensive or time-consuming techniques, such as lectures, self-directed training, or e-learning.
Excellent responses…	■ Suggest that Imani select which servers are shadowed so that new servers are learning from individuals who demonstrate strong job performance. Students may also suggest incentivizing the role of a trainer.
	■ Suggest ways for servers to learn off the job (e.g., giving servers a menu to review outside of work) or ways to distribute practice (e.g., having servers focus on smaller portions of the menu throughout their training).
	■ Suggest ways for servers to practice their knowledge and receive feedback (e.g., short quizzes on the menu; entering fake tickets into the cash register).
	■ Discuss or ask about other issues that aren't specifically about training, such as why there is high turnover, whether the selection measures are appropriate, and other related personnel issues.

EVALUATING "APPLICATION QUESTIONS"

1. Imagine you are working in a company that has had some difficulties with employees making racially insensitive comments or jokes. However, employees view going to diversity training as a punishment that only racist people require. How might you convince employees of the benefits of training? What might be some activities the company could do to help employees think more carefully about their comments?

   Evaluation Guide: Students may vary in their responses. However, you can identify some of the points in discussion:

   - Social psychology suggests we are all blind to some of our biases. Even individuals who believe they are not racist can make offensive or biased comments from time to time. Employees may be more receptive to this training if they perceive it as something that can help them to do their job more effectively or more easily, rather than perceiving it as punishment.
   - Students are likely to come up with many suggested activities. Encourage your students to think of ways a trainer could bring awareness to unconscious biases, help trainees identify offensive and nonoffensive comments, and practice how to confront someone if they say something offensive. These training methods might include skits, videos, case studies, role plays, or other innovative activities.
   - It will be important for the organization to ensure that employees are encouraged (not punished) for using their training. For example, if an employee speaks up about a racist joke, it will be important that that employee not be punished for speaking up. It also will be helpful for the organization to check in and see if people are using their training, and remembering/applying what they have learned.

2. According to some media sources, employers report that new graduates lack adequate critical thinking, communication, and time management skills when they begin their first jobs. Is there any truth to this complaint? What might universities do to better help students prepare for the work world? What can students do to prepare themselves? What might make it difficult for new graduates to transfer what they have learned at school to the workplace?

   Evaluation Guide: This may be a topic students have heard a lot about, especially in articles and reports that discuss the "millennial generation." Student responses may vary, but below are some possible avenues of discussion:

   - Universities can help make links between school and work more clear. Having clear learning outcomes, identifying the skills that students will get from courses, and providing opportunities to apply new knowledge in realistic scenarios can help students build these skills. In addition, clear expectations, firm deadlines, and using more active approaches (group projects, role plays, case studies, or other applied activities) are also approaches that can help students learn.

- Students can also take a more active role in their own education by finding ways to apply and share their new knowledge, trying to build skills on their own, recognizing that there is not always one right answer and that they should investigate alternatives, and holding themselves accountable for their own development. Many students benefit from practice with writing professional e-mails, working in groups, and meeting deadlines, all of which will be expected in the professional world.

3. Think of a time when you overlearned something. How did it happen? How did that overlearning become useful?

   Evaluation Guide: Students will have a variety of ideas, but the following examples might help prompt them if they have trouble getting started:
   - Driving a car is something that most people have overlearned. This usually happens because they get a great deal of practice and because most driving actions are fairly routine. This is useful because we can talk and think about other things while driving.
   - Some people have overlearned typing to such an extent that they can type and talk at the same time. People who do this can work more quickly; they are also able to plan what they will write because they don't need to concentrate on their typing.
   - Data entry can also be overlearned; when people have to type in the same information over and over again, they can often hold conversations or think about other tasks because they don't need to concentrate as much.
   - It might also be worthwhile to distinguish between multitasking and overlearning. Often we think we are effective at doing many things at once, like studying and playing on a computer, but research suggests this is not the case.

4. Imagine an organization has provided training on teamwork skills to their employees, and a subsequent knowledge test indicates the employees have learned what they are supposed to. However, these employees are not using their skills on the job—they speak rudely to teammates and sometimes fail to do their share of the work. What might be the issue? How could you address the problem?

   Evaluation Guide: Student responses may include some of the following suggestions:
   - Does the organization appear to support the transfer of learning? If the CEO or other leaders continue to engage in poor teamwork behaviors, it may make it seem to other employees that the training is not important, or that poor teamwork behaviors are actually accepted within the organization.
   - Are employees able to identify when they need to be using these skills? If the training appears to only measure learning and not behaviors (per Kirkpatrick's model), it could be that these employees are not learning how to actually engage in good team behaviors, or that they have trouble identifying when they should be using these behaviors.
   - What is the outcome when employees engage in good communication behaviors? If it makes their work more difficult or slower to complete, this also might discourage them from using the behaviors they have learned.

- There are a number of ways to approach this problem, including speaking with employees to see what prevents them from working with their teams, establishing ways for teams to hold one another accountable for their behaviors, tying rewards or promotion to team behaviors, or other approaches.

5. I/O practitioners are often confronted with training programs that have been created without much thought for ensuring that the training is accessible to minority groups. What might be one step you, as a consultant, could take to make training more accessible to an individual who is (a) elderly? (b) vision-impaired? (c) from a different country?

Evaluation Guide: Student responses may include some of the following suggestions:

- Elderly people may have less experience with technology, so offering face-to-face options might be helpful for them. In addition, given that elderly people may have hearing or vision difficulties, providing materials that can overcome these issues (e.g., large print, earphones where they can control volume, subtitles) can also be helpful.
- Most students will identify accommodations such as readers or braille materials. However, note that there are many times when training might convey information through videos, demonstrations, or similar tools that would need to be described for someone with vision impairments. Even color-coded information can be difficult for people with colorblindness to follow.
- There are several challenges that you may need to anticipate for an individual from a different country. The individual may not be an English speaker and might require translation of materials. Sometimes examples may be relevant to an individual from one country, but not another, such as examples that use foods, sports, or cultural references that the individual may not be familiar with, or idioms, such as "It's raining cats and dogs," that may confuse non-native English speakers.

HIGHLIGHTED STUDY FOR DISCUSSION

Truxillo, D. M., Paronto, M. E., Collins, M., & Sulzer, J. L. (2004). Effects of subject matter expert viewpoint on job analysis results. *Public Personnel Management, 33*, 33–46.

This article investigates how different sources of job analysis information (job incumbents versus consumers) differ in how they rate task importance. This is a good article for students to read because it is relatively short and straightforward in its methodology and statistics. Main points include the following:

- The researchers sampled ratings of a number of writing skills on police reports. As SMEs, they used police officers (the job incumbents) and district attorneys (who ultimately consume the police reports while building a case in court). It may be useful to initially present only the introduction and method to students so that you can discuss what they think will happen: Why might ratings differ for police officers and DAs?

- The researchers sampled 72 training officers and 33 DAs. The researchers asked participants to rate how critical 16 different writing skills are for writing effective police reports. These 16 skills were broken down into two dimensions: grammatical skills (such as using appropriate sentence structure) and content skills (such as recording all pertinent details).
- Using a 2 (occupation) × 2 (dimension) ANOVA indicates a main effect of occupation, a main effect of dimension, and an interaction between the two variables. Specifically, both DAs and police officers tend to consider content to be quite important; however, police officers believe that grammatical correctness is more important than do DAs.
- It would be useful to discuss the concept of accuracy: When ratings differ, how can we determine which is more accurate? It might also help to discuss more recent research that suggests that the SMEs' own experiences and personality can tint their view of job tasks.

WEB LEARNING

Title	Address
Association for Talent Development	https://www.td.org/
Training magazine	http://www.trainingmag.com
Training Time: Portal to training links	http://www.trainingtime.com
Training ABC: Training video/book store	http://www.trainingabc.com
Workforce Diversity Network	http://www.workforcediversitynetwork.com
HR Guide: Training Needs Analysis	http://www.hr-guide.com/data/G510.htm
Workforce magazine: Training and development community	http://www.workforce.com/index.html
McDonald's Hamburger University	http://www.aboutmcdonalds.com/mcd/careers/hamburger_university.html
Instructional Design website	http://www.instructionaldesign.org
International Coach Federation	http://www.coachfederation.org
International Journal of Training and Development	http://www.wiley.com/WileyCDA/WileyTitle/productCd-IJTD.html
The Thiagi Group	http://www.thiagi.com/

CHAPTER 9

Motivation

This chapter should help students understand:

- The importance of work motivation to organizational psychology
- How the three major categories of motivation theories differ from each other
- The similarities and differences among the various need–motive–value theories of motivation
- How cognitive choice theories emphasize the rationality of human behavior
- The similarities and differences between equity theory and expectancy theory
- How important self-regulatory processes are to work behavior
- The major principles and findings with respect to goal-setting theory
- Why discrepancies are so important to goal-directed behavior
- The widespread use and success of organizational behavior management programs for improving motivation and performance
- How successful goal setting (including management by objectives) is as an applied technique for improving motivation and performance
- What job enrichment approaches have to offer organizations and the various ways in which enrichment can be employed
- The current trends with respect to job crafting and how individuals change and create jobs to better fit their needs and to serve the organization

Chapter Summary

Few topics in I/O psychology have been as thoroughly explored as work motivation. In the first part of this chapter, I presented the most commonly cited theories of work motivation; in the second part, I focused on applications of these theories to organizational problems. Three sets of theories were considered: need–motive–value theories, cognitive choice theories, and self-regulation theories. Although need–motive–value theories are no longer as well accepted by researchers and academics as they were 40 years ago, they are still popular in business settings. First, we discussed Maslow's hierarchy of needs; then we examined two approaches that are related to Maslow's work: ERG theory and two-factor theory. Job characteristics theory and cognitive evaluation theory were also considered in this category, as they clarify the different motivational potentials that are inherent in jobs and people.

Cognitive choice theories, which view motivation and behavior as rational processes rather than as a function of inherent needs or values, were discussed in terms of two important theories: equity theory and expectancy theory. The latter—presented in the context of VIE theory—was described as the most rational theory of them all. Each of its three components was discussed in terms of recent meta-analytic research on expectancy theory. The conclusion drawn was that these three components seem related to motivation, though not always in the multiplicative manner predicted by the theory.

Self-regulation theories were discussed last. In this context, goal-setting theory was presented as one of the simplest and most empirically supported models of work motivation. Social cognitive theories were described as extensions of goal-setting theory that provide potential explanations for why goals are so important to individual motivation and performance. All three sets of theories have received a great deal of attention in the literature, some of which was reviewed in the text.

In the second part of the chapter, I presented applications of motivation theories to organizations. OBM was discussed as a very successful technique (particularly in the area of improving organizational safety) that stems from reinforcement theory. A similar approach was followed with respect to goal setting and management by objectives. There appears to be a great deal of support for these goal-based interventions as well. Finally, I discussed job enrichment and its potential for organizational improvement. In addition, some of the more cutting-edge thinking around job crafting and idiosyncratic deals was presented, and a series of questions was generated that could drive future research.

TEACHING THE CHAPTER

Various theoretical perspectives on motivation are presented in the first part of this chapter. These perspectives should be somewhat familiar to students, who have likely been introduced to this information in a general-level psychology course. Students should find this material interesting because many of these theories have an intuitive appeal. However, this can also be a liability, as students may gloss over the material when studying for exams, believing that they are already familiar with the concepts. On the other hand, their familiarity with this material can be an advantage in terms of class discussion and debate. For example, a debate that may stimulate lively conversation could focus on why there is not more empirical support for many of these theories (which is also discussed in the chapter).

Be sure that you clearly present and discuss the pros and cons of these motivational theories, including why using theoretical frameworks with mixed empirical support might impact organizational practice (e.g., discuss with students how such frameworks might be problematic or advantageous). The exercises and assignments included in this section can help students apply this chapter's lessons after they are clear on the theories and related concepts presented in the first part of the chapter.

Applying motivational theories to organizational problems is the central theme of the second part of the chapter. Numerous cases that demonstrate the application of these perspectives are presented in the chapter. For more information, especially related to organizational behavior management, you may want to view these online references: http://www.safetyperformance.com (Safety Performance Solutions, a consulting firm led by Scott Geller, who has been involved in safety-based behavioral interventions, including the pizza delivery driver studies mentioned in the chapter) or http://www.ishn.com (Industrial Safety and Hygiene News, an excellent resource for current articles related to applications of organizational behavior management).

The exercises below will guide students in applying theoretical concepts to workplace problems and their own experiences. One exercise involves examining the link between job characteristics theory and a job description to determine how motivation and performance can be improved. Students will also consider how a need theory applies to a highly complex job—that of president of the United States. They also will examine their experiences with goal setting in light of what was learned from expectancy theory. In addition to these exercises, another way to expose students to an organizational motivation problem is to use case studies in course discussion; case studies might come from a source such as the *Harvard Business Review*. You can also identify a current issue in the popular press where employee motivation might be an issue (e.g., company-wide layoffs).

SUGGESTED EXERCISES AND ASSIGNMENTS

Job Characteristics Theory and TSA (Transportation Security Administration) Officers

Purpose Students will analyze the job of an airline security officer within the framework of Hackman and Oldham's job characteristics theory and then develop ways to improve the job by considering its core job dimensions, improvements in employee motivation, and the overall attractiveness of this job.

Instructions

- Divide the class into groups of four to six.
- The tragic events of September 11, 2001, led to an intense debate about the effectiveness of airport security around the world. At the center of this debate was the state of airport security personnel's qualifications and what could be done to increase their competence. In this exercise, students will consider this question themselves.
- Groups should be instructed to brainstorm the results of a job analysis for a TSA officer. They should generate a list of KSAOs and job tasks that are necessary for the performance of a typical TSA officer, based on their own experience traveling through airports. Because some students may not have had such experiences, make the O★NET Transportation Security Screener description available (go to O★NET Online, job code #33-9093.00, at http://www.onetonline.org/link/summary/33-9093.00). Groups may also want to include a general description of the security screening process to assist in job redesign conversations.

- After the groups have generated their job analysis information, they should consider how this job fits (or does not fit) with job characteristics theory. Textbook Figure 9.3 illustrates the framework of the theory. Students should consider the extent to which a TSA officer experiences the following:
  - *Skill variety:* the extent to which an employee would perform the same functions during and across workdays
  - *Task identity:* the extent to which an employee can point to something from his or her work as being generated by personal effort
  - *Task significance:* the extent to which work tasks are perceived as important to coworkers and society
  - *Autonomy:* the extent to which an employee can make decisions and perform the job without approval or intrusion from supervisors
  - *Feedback:* the extent to which an employee receives information about the quality of work performance
  - *Experienced meaningfulness:* the extent to which an employee perceives the outcomes of his or her job as meaningful
  - *Responsibility for outcomes:* the extent to which the job generates a feeling of accountability in an employee
  - *Knowledge of results:* the extent to which an employee is aware of the outcomes of his or her efforts
- Students should prioritize the job characteristics according to the extent to which they need to be changed or not changed. They should provide the rationale behind the order of their rankings.
- Post the groups' rankings of the job characteristics and base your class discussion on these rankings. Are there any similarities or differences between groups?

Discussion Questions

- Do you see any issues with this job that fall outside the scope of job characteristics theory?
- How practical are the changes that you have proposed?
- Would you make the same changes to improve *performance* as you would to improve *motivation*?
- Is there anything that passengers could do that would improve the motivation of TSA officers?

Self-Actualization and the Commander-in-Chief

Purpose Students will consider the job of president of the United States (or leader of another country, if applicable) in light of Maslow's hierarchy of needs. In doing so, they will also find themselves discussing the positive and negative facets of a job that holds great power, prestige, and responsibility.

Instructions

- Current articles available in popular magazines (e.g., *Newsweek, Time*), presidential biographies, or television shows may provide valuable information for this exercise.

- This exercise is well suited for use with the entire class.
- Have the class discuss the job of president and its potential for personal need fulfillment.
  - Remind students that Maslow's hierarchy proposes that one can self-actualize only after lower-level needs are fulfilled. You may want to direct students to Figure 9.1, which depicts the five levels of the hierarchy.
  - Keep students focused on the need levels: physiological, safety, love, esteem, and self-actualization.
- After the class has discussed the potential for self-actualization, you could split the class into two groups—one that believes the presidency can lead to self-actualization and one that believes it cannot. Ensure that the discussion includes the reasons why students feel one way or the other.

Discussion Questions

- How well does Maslow's hierarchy apply to a job as complex as that of president?
- Would our debate differ if we were using Alderfer's ERG framework as the basis of our analysis? If so, how?
- What historical figures do you believe achieved self-actualization? What makes you think so?

Explaining Behavior Using Expectancy Theory

Purpose This exercise will allow students to consider how their own values, instrumentalities, and expectancies have interacted and played a role in motivating past actions or inactions.

Instructions

- Give students 10 minutes to recall and write down one example of attaining a goal and one example of failing to attain a goal. (The goal could be anything that is personally meaningful—academic, sports-related, etc.) For both examples, they should analyze how their values, perceptions of instrumentality, and expectancies interacted to affect their success (or lack of success).
- Divide the class into groups of four to six to discuss their experiences.
- Have groups attempt to identify which component of expectancy theory seemed to be most significant overall in group members' goal attainment and failure to achieve their goals.
- Facilitate discussion of the three components of goal attainment and how they may influence behavior.

Discussion Questions

- Do the components of expectancy theory seem to affect people at the same stage of the decision-making processes related to goal attainment?
- Would knowledge of expectancy theory have helped you reach a goal that you did not achieve? If so, how?

Learning How to Set Goals

Purpose Students will apply goal-setting theory to a behavior relevant to their own lives.

Instructions

- Have students work with a partner to create a goal that is relevant to them. This goal may be related to school or work (e.g., studying more for class or learning something new) or to something in their personal life (e.g., exercising more).
- Give students a few minutes to write down an initial goal. Next, discuss aspects of an effective goal; a common acronym to help design goals is SMART— goals should be specific, measurable, attainable, relevant, and timely (Doran, 1981).
- Have students trade statements with their partner to get feedback. You may also want to check in with students to see how they are doing. For example, you could prompt a student who writes down "Exercise more" to be more specific, such as "Exercise for 30 minutes at least three times a week."
- You might check in with students later on to see whether this approach was effective for them.

Discussion Questions

- When you create a specific goal for yourself, does this specificity make it seem easier to achieve? Why or why not?
- What are some ways you can remind yourself of your goal? What can you do if you fail to reach your goal or if you fall behind in your progress?
- What are some other examples of goal setting that you or others have used to achieve something?

Looking Back: How Do We Improve Secondary Education?

Purpose Students will use their educational backgrounds to consider what might enrich the experiences of the next generation of high school students.

Instructions

- Divide the class into small groups and lead them through this exercise by following these steps:
    - Describe your typical high school educational environment.
    - What parts of your high school education were particularly motivating? What was lacking in this regard? Consider these questions within the context of the motivational theories that were just presented to you.
    - Based on your experiences, the motivational theories, and the principles of learning you have reviewed, how would you enrich the high school education you described in the first step of this exercise? Any suggestions you offer should be supported by motivational theories and principles of learning.

Discussion Questions

- What did you learn from one another about different styles of high school education? What were the noticeable differences in your fellow students' educational backgrounds?
- What educational experiences were common to most of you?
- Were there any motivational areas that all of you agreed needed some type of change? If so, what were they?
- In your opinion, what are the most important characteristics in a motivational environment?

EVALUATING "TAKING IT TO THE FIELD"

Poor responses...	■ Provide a superficial response to the advice (e.g., "These sound great!").
	■ Indicate that the suggestions are not good but fail to clearly critique the problems with the suggestions.
	■ Provide a critique of only one of the suggestions.
	■ Fail to provide an additional suggestion for motivating employees or provide an approach that has little empirical support (e.g., Maslow's hierarchy of needs) or misapplies an approach.
Good responses...	■ Identify at least one error in the advice regarding job characteristics model:
	■ The advice suggests reducing task variety; in fact, the job characteristics model suggests that increasing task variety will increase motivation.
	■ The advice also suggests adhering strictly to a set handbook. This also goes against the job characteristics model of autonomy; tour guides will likely be more motivated if they have some control over how they do their job and if they can change their approach based on their tour group.
	■ Part of the job characteristics model is concerned with whether an individual has high growth need strength. It might be helpful for Blues Bus Tours to provide tour guides with high growth need strength by means of more opportunities to make the work feel meaningful. For example, tour guides could receive feedback from their tour group, be given more autonomy in how they conduct tours, or be offered a variety of tours they could lead to keep things interesting for them.
	■ Identify at least one error in the advice regarding paying employees more:

■ Equity theory does not suggest that paying employees more leads to motivation. Specifically, equity theory is based on comparisons between the self and others. In this scenario, there is no comparison between individuals, so it is unclear if employees feel inequitably treated. In fact, paying everyone more means that people who don't work hard will get a raise too, so this strategy will not address the problem. Furthermore, there is little empirical evidence supporting the assertion that overpayment leads to guilt on the part of the employee, which leads to harder work. Instead, individuals typically make justifications for their overpayment.

■ Likewise, this is a misapplication of two-factor theory. In this case, pay is a hygiene factor, which means that the lack of pay will lead to dissatisfaction, but an increase in pay will not lead to motivation.

■ Suggest an additional approach, but it may have mixed empirical support (e.g., Herzberg's two-factor theory) or may not provide enough detail to demonstrate that the student has a strong understanding of how to apply the theory.

Excellent responses...

■ Identify at least one error in the advice regarding job characteristics model:

■ The advice suggests reducing task variety. In fact, the job characteristics model suggests that increasing task variety will increase motivation.

■ The advice also suggests adhering strictly to a set handbook. This also goes against the job characteristics model of autonomy; tour guides will likely be more motivated if they have some control over how they do their job and if they can change their approach based on each tour group they encounter.

■ The job characteristics model is concerned in part with whether or not an individual has high growth need strength. It might be helpful for Blues Bus Tours to provide tour guides with high growth need strength by means of more opportunities to make the work feel meaningful. For example, tour guides could receive feedback from their tour group, be given more autonomy in how they conduct tours, or be offered a variety of tours to lead as a way of keeping the work interesting and engaging for them.

■ Strong responses may also link additional theories to refute this advice. For example, the lack of autonomy prevents any opportunities for job crafting, which has been found to be beneficial for motivation. ERG theory and SDT also note the value of growth and autonomy, which is prevented by this advice.

- Identify at least one error in the advice regarding paying employees more:
  - Equity theory does not suggest that paying employees more leads to motivation. Specifically, equity theory is based on comparisons between the self and others. In this scenario, there is no comparison between individuals, so it is unclear if employees feel inequitably treated. In fact, paying everyone more means that people who don't work hard will get a raise too, so this strategy will not address the problem. Furthermore, there is little empirical evidence supporting the assertion that overpayment leads to guilt on the part of the employee, which leads to harder work. Instead, individuals typically make justifications for their overpayment.
  - Likewise, this is a misapplication of two-factor theory. In this case, pay is a hygiene factor, which means that the lack of pay will lead to dissatisfaction, but an increase in pay will not lead to motivation.
  - Strong responses may also cite evidence from other theories that refutes this recommendation. For example, the over-justification effect suggests that higher pay may not help with intrinsic motivation, so in the end, the workers may not be more motivated to do their jobs despite the higher pay. Similarly, the fact that all employees are getting raises may cause problems according to justice theory—if workers see their lazy colleagues receive raises with no clear justification or explanation, it may seem like lazy employees are being rewarded for their laziness. Linking raises with performance would be more effective.
- Suggest an additional approach that has strong empirical support (e.g., the job characteristics model or goal setting) and provide enough detail on how the approach should be applied to make it clear that the student understands how the theory works.

EVALUATING "APPLICATION QUESTIONS"

1. Imagine you have a friend who is currently dissatisfied with her job. She feels that she puts a great deal of effort and time into her job yet is passed over for promotions and awards. What would you suggest she do to feel more motivated about her job?

   Evaluation Guide: Students are likely to have a number of suggestions. You are likely to see some of the following responses:
   - Your friend could stop putting so much effort into her work or find other ways to limit her input (e.g., not offering as much of her expertise).

- Your friend could change her outcomes by asking for a raise, a promotion, or some other valuable reward.
- Your friend could change her comparison group. If people who are getting promoted are much older and more experienced than she is, she may be unreasonable in her expectations and should examine her input/outputs vis-à-vis a group that is more similar to her.

2. Interview a friend, family member, or associate about his or her work environment. Consider the three needs for optimal health and well-being, as described in Ryan and Deci's self-determination theory: *competence, relatedness,* and *autonomy.* Based on your interview, what interventions would you recommend to this person's employer to meet these needs?

   Evaluation Guide: Students will likely have many ideas for how these three components could be addressed:
   - In terms of competence, students will likely talk about experiences that allow someone to practice skills and allow them to develop skills further. Examples might include having orientation activities for new employees, offering training or development opportunities, and allowing employees to engage in activities that they feel fit their talents and abilities.
   - In terms of relatedness, employers can find many ways to help employees feel more connected, such as mentorship programs, picnics or other socials, interest clubs, and company celebrations, such as holiday parties or summer barbeques.
   - In terms of autonomy, suggestions will likely depend very much on the job. In some positions (such as manufacturing jobs) there may be limited autonomy, and little way to change this. In other jobs, however, students might talk about the ability to job craft or to work on interdepartmental teams on a project where employees can lend their expertise and make decisions about how to carry out projects.

3. Consider the job of a babysitter. Based on control theory, what are some examples of feedback that they might look for to determine whether they're doing a good job? Where might they look to find a "standard" for babysitters that they can compare to their own behaviors to determine whether they are successful?

   Evaluation Guide: Students may note that feedback for babysitters may not be forthcoming—it is possible that parents simply stop calling them, rather than give them feedback. However, babysitters who want to be proactive might look for a "standard" for babysitters—perhaps a peer who has a good reputation as a babysitter, a childhood sitter that the individual remembers fondly, or a babysitter from a movie or a book (such as the *Babysitters Club* children's books). The babysitter then might compare him/herself to that standard, and see where they don't live up to this standard. For example, other babysitters might bring along toys, games, or coloring books to engage the children; if a babysitter realizes that she spends most of her time ignoring the children and texting with her friends, she might realize that she is not meeting a standard, and may be motivated to change her behaviors to be more in-line with those of the standard. Examples of this will vary, but most will follow this pattern.

4. The manager of a graphic design studio wants to improve the quality of his company's output. He decides he is going to set a goal for his staff: "We will make $100,000 in commissions within the next three months." What are some problems with his goal? What would you suggest as a more effective goal?

   Evaluation Guide: As noted in the text, goals are best when they are specific and difficult (but achievable) and when you receive feedback about progress. Thus, responses may include the following:

   - This goal is not very specific—it does not relate to a behavior that the friend has control over. Instead of making the goal about reaching a specific commission (which he has little control over), it could be about reaching out to a certain number of clients to build a relationship, or spending time each day developing a list of individuals to solicit for business.
   - This goal is also not necessarily achievable—making such a high commission may be too difficult. The manager may instead want to set a more reasonable goal, or more intermediate goals (e.g., $10,000 in one month, with a goal of $30,000 over three months).
   - Finally, it will be difficult for the manager to receive feedback along the way— he will only know if his team has met the goal at the end of three months. Having a more specific goal with smaller intermediary steps will help him adjust his behaviors along the way. For example, meeting with his team to check in, and going along for sales pitches might help him see what behaviors are lacking and will help him adjust his team's approach before the three months are up.

5. A company has fired a department manager after repeated complaints from his staff that he failed to meet with them for performance reviews or provide them with adequate feedback on their work. The new manager wants to use the i-deals model to build a better supervisor–subordinate relationship with her team. What are some challenges she might face in instituting this new system? What ways might she be able to overcome these challenges?

   Evaluation Guide: This scenario is broad, and so students are likely to come up with a wide array of responses. The following are a few examples.

   - In terms of challenges she might face, this new manager may need to deal with the aftereffects of the previous manager. The subordinates may be hesitant to trust her, or may be skeptical of the new system. They also may have little idea of what their level of performance was due to the lack of feedback from the previous manager, so they may have difficulty making decisions about how to do the work. In addition, sometimes the things employees want are not feasible in a certain workplace (e.g., options for telework).
   - In order to overcome these difficulties, the new manager can be very clear about what expectations everyone has for one another, and what her standards are for the work. However, if she is able to also find ways to give regular, objective feedback, and help employees work on their personal development, her employees may gradually become more accustomed to the i-deal approach to work.

6. Job crafting is a relatively new idea in the field. What are some advantages of allowing employees to customize their own jobs? What are some disadvantages? Have you had opportunities to craft your own job?

Evaluation Guide: Because research is still developing in this area, students may come up with a number of ideas for which we have not yet found empirical support. Example answers may include the following:

- *Advantages:* People can focus on tasks they enjoy and are good at; people can work on their own to match the work to their values and interests; people can work to develop their self-efficacy; people can set their own goals and pace, which may help them feel more satisfied.

- *Disadvantages:* People who are not motivated may craft their job in such a way that they can expend minimal effort to meet the requirements; some people may feel anxious when faced with such an ambiguous job; some people may not have a good understanding of what behaviors contribute to the goals of the organization.

- Examples of personal job crafting might include doing well enough that a manager allows them to take on extra tasks they find interesting, or sharing a job with a colleague who has a talent in an area they are less skilled in.

HIGHLIGHTED STUDY FOR DISCUSSION

Latham, G. P., & Baldes, J. J. (1975). The "practical significance" of Locke's theory of goal setting. *Journal of Applied Psychology, 60,* 122–124.

Although this is quite an old article, it is an excellent example of bridging the scientist/practitioner gap. It also is short and accessible to students with little experience in reading psychology research articles. The main points of the article are as follows:

- The authors set out to demonstrate the practical value of goal setting in a field setting. Weyerhauser Company, a paper mill, was experiencing problems with the way that logging trucks were loaded—many trucks were being loaded well below capacity, causing the trucks to take more trips, which was a waste of time, wages, and fuel.

- Prior to the experiment, when the truckers were asked to "do their best" at loading trucks as close to the maximum weight as possible, they were loading trucks to only about 60% of capacity.

- The authors set the difficult but attainable goal of having trucks loaded to over 90% capacity. Almost immediately, trucks were being loaded to about 80% capacity, which increased over time to about 94% capacity. This high performance was maintained even after the researchers ended their observations. Ultimately, this change in behaviors saved the company $250,000 over the course of nine months.

WEB LEARNING

Title	Address
Abraham Maslow: Information and publications	http://www.maslow.com
Changing Minds.org: Motivation theories	http://changingminds.org/explanations/theories/a_motivation.htm
My Skills Profile: Motivation Questionnaire	http://www.myskillsprofile.com/tests/mq
Your Coach: Summary of Major Motivation Theories	http://www.yourcoach.be/en/employee-motivation-theories/
Inc. Magazine's Guide to Motivating Employees	http://www.inc.com/guides/hr/20776.html
Organizational Behavior Division of the Academy of Management	http://obweb.org
Organization and Management Theory Division of the Academy of Management	http://omtweb.org/
Organization Development Network	http://www.odnetwork.org

Job Attitudes: Antecedents and Consequences

Chapter Summary

This chapter is divided into four sections. The first section presented some background information on attitudes, behaviors, and the relationship among them. At the outset, the theory of planned behavior, a model of this relationship, was discussed and then referred to throughout, with an emphasis on the links between work-related attitudes and organizational outcomes. The work of Ajzen and Fishbein provided a nice foundation for the more work-specific issues that were discussed later in the chapter.

Second, after a consideration of various reasons why I/O researchers and practitioners are interested in job attitudes, a detailed overview of job satisfaction was presented, using Figure 10.2 as a basis for discussion. Research was cited that deals with the four main classes of antecedents to job satisfaction: job characteristics, individual/personal characteristics, social factors, and growth opportunities. All of these antecedents appear to make important contributions to employees' levels of job satisfaction. A few scales that measure job satisfaction were discussed, examples of those scales were included, and the multidimensional nature of job satisfaction was considered. In the conclusion to this section on job satisfaction, three classes of organizational outcome variables (consequences) that appear to be substantively linked to job satisfaction were discussed at length: performance, withdrawal behaviors, and counterproductive behaviors.

In the third section, Figure 10.10 was presented as a working heuristic for the discussion of organizational commitment. Throughout, the text reviewed Meyer and Allen's three-component model: affective commitment, continuance commitment, and normative commitment. The antecedents of organizational commitment were classified as organizational, individual, or social in nature. Each of these sets of variables seems to have potential effects on organizational commitment. Indeed, recent research in this area demonstrates that performance, withdrawal behaviors, and counterproductive behaviors are all influenced by organizational commitment. Organizational profiles were examined as a newer focus of commitment research. Finally, the chapter ended with a discussion of other work attitudes, including job involvement, work centrality, perceived organizational support, and emotions in the workplace, with a particular focus on the regulation of emotions in the workplace.

TEACHING THE CHAPTER

As discussed in this chapter, the study of work attitudes is important for a number of reasons. Work attitudes are related to a variety of organizational outcomes and are an appropriate focus for I/O psychologists who select, train, and evaluate employees. In addition, work attitudes affect our professional lives as well as our personal lives and well-being. Work attitudes can make the work environment a better place. Job satisfaction and organizational commitment are the two primary work attitudes discussed extensively throughout this chapter. Facilitating discussion of these issues and soliciting examples from students whose work experiences should easily illustrate these concepts will nicely complement your lecture materials. A common assumption is that I/O psychology is the study of what makes people happy at work, and many people enter the field to research this topic and make a difference in society. In the business sections of libraries and bookstores, self-help books and various publications that deal strictly with job satisfaction, organizational commitment, and other specific work attitudes offer evidence for a general interest in work attitudes. This chapter is well suited to individuals with such interests.

Like many issues studied in psychology, attitudes are not directly observable. One may be able to infer an attitude from someone's behavior, but it is difficult to say with absolute certainty that an individual is committed to or satisfied with his or her job. Therefore, we use surveys to capture and understand these phenomena. This chapter includes some sample items from popular measures that have been used in practice and research. In the section that follows, there are some websites you may want to use as a background for a discussion on surveys.

Be sure to reinforce the previous class lessons about the importance of *reliability* and *validity* in assessing job attitudes, as well as the importance of asking questions that measure a single construct (e.g., affective commitment).

SUGGESTED EXERCISES AND ASSIGNMENTS

Are We Happy and Committed Employees? A Qualitative Investigation

Purpose The objective of this exercise is to have students explore the job characteristics they find important for determining their job satisfaction and organizational commitment.

Instructions

This exercise is meant to stimulate class discussion based on as many ideas and experiences as possible. Thus, it is recommended that you do not divide the class into groups (unless you have a very large class).

- Solicit suggestions from students about the aspects of a job that they have found make them:
  - Happy with the job
  - Unhappy with the job
  - Committed to their organization
  - Not committed to their organization
- After generating a list of job characteristics that have contributed to their job satisfaction/dissatisfaction and commitment/lack of commitment, categorize the characteristics with regard to the frameworks for job satisfaction (Figure 10.2) and organizational commitment (Figure 10.10) provided in the text.
- What themes emerged during the discussion? Discuss what they mean for students when they are searching for a job; also discuss what students look for in organizations when they are considering the requirements and retention policies for jobs.

Discussion Questions

- Why do we pay attention to the factors that make us unhappy? Why not just pay attention to the ones that make us happy? Do you recall what motivation theory also makes this distinction?
- What job characteristics seem to affect both job satisfaction and organizational commitment?
- Are there factors that seem to affect job satisfaction more than organizational commitment? Organizational commitment more than job satisfaction?

Are We Happy and Committed Employees?
A Quantitative Investigation

Purpose The objective of this exercise is to have students explore the job characteristics they find important for determining their job satisfaction and organizational commitment. It can be used in place of the previous qualitative exercise or in conjunction with it to show the value of quantitative versus qualitative data.

Instructions

- Prior to class, ask students to fill out some measures of job satisfaction as well as any other outcomes that might relate to satisfaction. Some possible measures could include the following:
  - The Job Descriptive Index (JDI), which is available for free from http://www.bgsu.edu/arts-and-sciences/psychology/graduate-program/industrial-organizational/research/job-descriptive-index.html and measures facets of satisfaction
  - The Job in General scale (JIG), available from the same website, measures overall satisfaction
  - Other available measures assess motivation, happiness, stress, or other relevant outcomes
- Score the tests, and calculate correlations between each facet and overall satisfaction as well as any other outcome variables you assessed.
- Share the results of these analyses with students. In small classes, you may need to note that the small sample size makes the estimates unstable; in larger classes, typically satisfaction with work itself is most strongly related to overall satisfaction. In addition, satisfaction with pay as well as with opportunities for promotion are typically quite low among students.
- If you also used the previous exercise, you could compare the results of the empirical evidence with students' qualitative responses. Often, what students believe is most important to their satisfaction is not what actually relates to overall performance once the different facets are assessed.

Discussion Questions

- What facets appear to be most important to overall satisfaction? Why might that be?
- What facets appear to be low for this sample? Why might this be the case? Is this problematic, or is it simply a fact of life for college students?
- Which of these facets would likely be the easiest to change? The hardest?
- How do these results match qualitative results? How do they differ?

Are Work Attitudes Important in Organizational Life?

Purpose The objective of this exercise is to have students consider the importance of work attitudes in organizational life.

Instructions

- This exercise can be used in place of a lecture to emphasize the importance of work attitudes.
- *Prior to class:* Have students search popular press (newspapers, newsmagazine, etc.) websites for information about an organization. The organization should be one that students think is doing a good/poor job in keeping employees satisfied and/or committed.
- During class, ask students to discuss the following questions:
  - What made you select this organization?
  - Do you think that job attitudes such as job satisfaction and organizational behavior influence work behavior in this organization?
  - How does this organization affect its employees' attitudes? If the organization is doing a poor job of keeping its employees satisfied/committed, what costs may it face if it fails to consider worker attitudes?
  - Did you find information about the organization that demonstrates it promotes job satisfaction or encourages commitment?
  - Do you think our job-related attitudes affect our overall attitudes about life outside of the workplace (e.g., attitudes about friends, family)?
- Have students lead the class discussion by presenting their answers to these questions in a way that builds a case for the importance of work attitudes in organizational functioning.

Discussion Questions

- Overall, do you think that attitudes are important to organizations?
- What do you think happens when employees collectively are dissatisfied with their job/the organization? What are the positive outcomes for an organization with satisfied employees?
- How would you build job satisfaction in employees working in this organization? How would you improve organizational commitment?

Hiring a Capable Airline Ticket Counter Agent

Purpose The objective of this exercise is to have students design a screening system for a job that requires a high level of customer service and the ability to regulate emotions.

Instructions

- Divide the class into small groups of four to six students.
- Ask groups to design a system that effectively screens airline ticket counter agents based on their emotion regulation ability.
  - You may find it helpful to have the O★NET job description for Reservation and Transportation Ticket Agents and Travel Clerks available (go to O★NET online, job title #43-4181.00, at http://online.onetcenter .org/link/summary/43-4181.00).

- The primary job task for this position is to interface with the public, which makes it an ideal candidate for an exercise involving emotion regulation.
- Giving students very few guidelines should enhance their creativity in this exercise. Remind them of the information they have learned thus far in the course (e.g., recruitment, selection, training). Assessment tools may include anything from a paper-and-pencil test to an assessment center to any other instrument that may effectively differentiate candidates who can regulate their emotions from those who cannot.
- Have groups justify their chosen selection tool by linking its use to the job. Also, ask students to indicate how their assessment would be scored (and weighted, if using more than one methodology).
- Have groups present their selection systems to the class.

Discussion Questions

- Did you encounter any difficulty trying to assess emotion regulation?
- What role does training play in how employees perform emotional labor on the job?
- Does your selection system apply to other customer service–oriented jobs or is this job unique?

Job Characteristics

Purpose The objective of this exercise is to have students connect what they have learned about Hackman and Oldham's job characteristics model from Chapter 4 to job attitudes.

Instructions

- Ask students to consider a job they are familiar with or one that is likely to have a number of dissatisfied employees. Some examples might include the following:
  - A factory worker who does the same monotonous task all day, every day
  - A social worker who never finds out what happens to the people she helps
  - A dog trainer who never knows whether his clients continue to work with the dog after he finishes with them
  - A pizza delivery driver who works in a town where people don't tip well
- Ask students to use the job characteristics model to determine ways they might change the job itself to increase satisfaction. For example, students might suggest ways that organizations can show workers how their efforts matter.

Discussion Questions

- Which job characteristics seem easiest to change? Most difficult?
- Which job characteristic do you believe is most important to worker satisfaction? Why?
- Do you believe we always have control over job characteristics? Why or why not?

EVALUATING "TAKING IT TO THE FIELD"

The Chapter 10 activity involves a decrease in morale among bank employees who have experienced a layoff at another location. The client, Karen Strazinski, believes the employees are afraid for their own jobs, even though she has assured them they are safe. She also believes some of the employees at the recently closed Green River branch who transferred to her South Bend branch are spreading rumors and making other employees anxious. Students can have a variety of effective responses to the prompt. Below are some suggestions for grading the responses.

Poor responses...	■ Suggest that Karen continue to do what she is doing, or suggest that she send a sharp e-mail to employees about their performance.
	■ Fail to provide Karen with specific actions she can take to help increase morale for employees.
	■ Overlook the problem of withdrawal among employees.
	■ Provide only one or two suggestions to Karen, and do not recognize that satisfaction relates to more than just the closure of the branch.
	■ Assert that it is now too late to address the problem.
Good responses...	■ Use proper spelling and grammar.
	■ Indicate that employees are engaging in withdrawal behaviors, which indicate dissatisfaction with the job.
	■ Recognize that job satisfaction can be approached in several ways—for example, a good response might note that perceived organizational support may be lacking and that job characteristics may also be influencing worker satisfaction.
	■ Provide concrete suggestions for how Karen can handle the situation—for example, having a discussion with employees explaining the closure of the Green River branch and why this does not mean the South Bend branch will also be closed.
	■ Recommend that Karen *not* send a sharp e-mail and instead communicate face-to-face with her employees in a friendly manner.
Excellent responses...	■ Use flawless spelling and grammar.
	■ Recognize that employees are engaging in withdrawal behaviors, and connect that to both a lack of satisfaction and to issues of motivation.
	■ Connect their recommendations with what they have learned in both Chapter 9 and Chapter 10. For example, an excellent response might note that employees may feel that they are being treated unjustly, so Karen might provide informational and interactional justice in her discussions about the closure of the Green River branch.

- ▪ Identify several ways that Karen can approach job satisfaction, including examining how job characteristics, social factors, growth opportunities, commitment, involvement, positive organizational support, and/or emotional labor might be affecting attitudes.
- ▪ Recommend that Karen communicate face-to-face with her employees in a sensitive manner, as suggested by justice theory.
- ▪ Suggest that Karen target the transfer employees in particular. They are likely still acclimating to the new branch and likely have a great deal of anxiety about whether they will also lose this job. Karen should find ways to help them socialize with fellow employees and work hard to ensure that they feel supported by their new organization.

EVALUATING "APPLICATION QUESTIONS"

1. Compare two jobs you have held and your overall satisfaction with those jobs. Was your satisfaction similar in both jobs? If so, why do you think that is? If not, what affected your satisfaction?

   Evaluation Guide: This question gets at the heart of whether job satisfaction is related to the individual or the workplace. Your students will likely express a variety of responses. Discussion points might include the following:
   - ▪ Many students will have had temporary jobs that paid poorly and offered little in the way of promotion. Thus, if they find they have similar attitudes across jobs, it may be useful to discuss whether they feel they are currently building a career versus just working at a series of unrelated and unimportant jobs.
   - ▪ Because affectivity is related to job attitudes, students who have strong positive or negative affect will likely have similar attitudes across jobs. So it might be useful to gauge students' attitudes toward a variety of topics to see if they are consistent in their attitudes in many arenas.
   - ▪ Students may say that their attitudes come from a particular aspect of a job— for example, they may discuss how they did not fit in a particular organization or how they had great coworkers and managers. This is a good opportunity to discuss how facets of job satisfaction relate to overall satisfaction as well as to other outcomes, such as citizenship behaviors or counterproductive work behaviors.

2. It is common in consulting work to encounter managers who believe that job attitudes do not matter—if someone quits, they will just hire another person to replace the departing employee. What might you say to these types of managers?

Evaluation Guide: This question gives students an opportunity to connect with other topics in the book. The following points may be relevant:

- Recruiting, selecting, and training new employees is expensive; if an organization can retain a good employee, this will save it money in the long run.
- In an unpleasant job, the organization may lose high-performing employees because they have more alternatives than low-performing ones. Thus, replacing a lost employee with a new employee will not guarantee that the new employee will be as good as the one who left.
- When an organization has high turnover, it is difficult to develop employees over time for promotion. As a result, upper-level managers may be external hires who will need training to learn about the organization and its culture.

3. Imagine you have to tell one of your best employees that she will not be getting her expected bonus check this year due to financial problems in the company. What might you tell her to ensure that she still feels satisfied with her job, even though she will be disappointed about her bonus check?

Evaluation Guide: This question is well addressed using the justice approach. Suggestions include the following:

- Providing this employee with a clear explanation for why she is not getting the bonus is key.
- Providing interactional justice is also helpful—expressing regret over the lost bonus will help her feel more supported.
- Finding ways to thank her for her work other than through monetary incentives may also help; for example, giving her an extra day off or giving her an award or some other recognition may help her feel valued and supported by the organization.

4. The chapter discusses emotional labor (when employees must fake positive emotions or hide negative emotions). Provide an example in which you had to engage in emotional labor and how that experience made you feel about that situation.

Evaluation Guide: Naturally, students will have a variety of stories to tell in response to this question. Some of the following points can be addressed:

- Many students work in service industries, where they are required to be kind to rude customers. You could ask them to discuss how they feel after dealing with a rude customer and how they might blow off steam afterward (e.g., complaining to coworkers).
- You could also ask about situations in which students had to do the opposite of typical emotional labor—that is, fake negative emotions or hide positive emotions. For example, police officers, property repossessors, and the like may need to act aggressively even when they are in a good mood. Similarly, people who work with children may need to respond sternly, even when it is amusing, when children engage in misbehavior.

- It is also worth discussing what happens if someone has had to engage in emotional labor constantly over a long period of time. What strategies do people use to make this process easier (e.g., attempting to actually experience the faked emotion rather than just faking it)?

5. If you were to win enough money in a lottery so that you would never need to work again if you didn't want to, would you still work? Why or why not?

Evaluation Guide: Students often like discussing this topic and have varying opinions about it. Essentially, this question is about work centrality—individuals who believe that work is a key part of their identity will continue to work despite not needing the money. Some potential discussion points might include the following:

- If some students would opt not to work, what do they think they would do with their free time? How would they meet new people and find ways to socialize if they don't have a job?
- Discuss what it is like to be out of work for a long time. Most students have not experienced a long period of unemployment and thus may not realize that they could become quite bored. Students who have had that experience may have interesting points to share with others.
- It could also be valuable to discuss how students might change their career plans if they did not need to work for the money. Would they choose a different, less lucrative career? How might they incorporate the skills and activities of that alternative career into their life now, given that they have not actually won the lottery?

HIGHLIGHTED STUDY FOR DISCUSSION

Yannis, G., Lange, T., & Tabvuma, V. (2012). The impact of life events on job satisfaction. *Journal of Vocational Behavior, 80,* 464–473.

This recent article examines the effect of life events (e.g., marriage, childbearing) on job satisfaction. It also complements the content of the book, in that the text indicates that the job itself affects satisfaction, as do individual differences. This article suggests that life events can affect job satisfaction above and beyond how stable individual differences affect satisfaction. The article can be particularly valuable for students who are inexperienced with research articles, as the results are presented in an easy-to-understand graphical form. Key points include the following:

- The authors assessed only first marriage and birth of the first child as "life events" that affect job satisfaction. You could ask students to come up with additional life events they believe are worth investigating (e.g., getting a divorce, buying a house, sending the first child to college). You might also have a discussion about the narrow definition of "life events" for this study—note that unmarried and childless individuals could not be included in this study because of the way life events are defined.

- The authors measure lead and lag variables: They have several lead variables that assess satisfaction up to four years prior to the life event. Likewise, they assess satisfaction up to five years and more after the life event.
- The authors control for a number of demographic variables, such as age, occupation, education, and the like. You could discuss with students what it means to "control" for variables and why certain variables are chosen to be controlled for. The authors also separate private- versus public-sector employees, as well as men and women—it could be helpful to discuss with students why these two variables might affect the findings.
- The results on marriage indicate that both men in the public sector and women in the private sector experience a boost in job satisfaction prior to marriage; men in the private sector and women in the public sector, meanwhile, experience a marked drop in satisfaction after marriage. It might be fruitful to discuss why this occurs.
- The results for the birth of a first child are more obvious; women in both the private and public sectors experience a notable drop in job satisfaction that can last more than five years. Men in the private sector also experience a gradual decrease in satisfaction over the course of five years.
- The results likely illustrate the difficulties associated with work–family conflict. Although marriage and the birth of children are often considered positive events, it is clear that they have a negative impact on satisfaction in the workplace. You could discuss with students what workplaces can do to help with this issue (or whether it is inevitable). It could also be interesting to discuss the differences between men and women, particularly with respect to child rearing, and why these differences might exist.

WEB LEARNING

Title	Address
Mayo Clinic: Job Satisfaction: How to make work more rewarding	http://www.mayoclinic.org/healthy-lifestyle/adult-health/in-depth/job-satisfaction/art-20046539
HRM Guide: Results from their job satisfaction survey	http://www.hrmguide.com/commitment/job-satisfaction.htm
Emotions Network (EMONET)	http://www.emotionsnet.org/
HRhero.com: Absenteeism and attendance of employees	http://www.hrhero.com/topics/absenteeism.html
WebMD: Are you a workaholic?	http://www.webmd.com/mental-health/features/workaholism
Bureau of Labor Statistics: Job Openings and Labor Turnover Survey	http://www.bls.gov/jlt/home.htm
University of Michigan Institute for Social Research: Survey Research Center	http://www.src.isr.umich.edu

CHAPTER 11

Stress and Worker Well-Being

LEARNING OBJECTIVES

This chapter should help students understand:

- The difference between stressors and strains
- How coping skills help individuals handle stress
- Warr's environmental determinants of well-being
- Many of the important issues that are involved in work–family conflict
- The importance of family-friendly employee benefits
- The ways in which companies are helping employees balance their work and family lives with as little stress as possible
- The particular complexities faced by dual-earner couples
- Why job loss and underemployment are among the most severe sources of stress that individuals ever experience
- The factors that trigger workplace violence in the United States today

Chapter Summary

The purpose of this chapter was to discuss stress as it manifests itself in the workplace. The chapter began with a look at stressors, strains, and coping. After defining these important terms and briefly considering stress in general, we looked at a model that indicates various sources and outcomes of job-related stress. In the second section, Warr's model of environmental determinants is discussed as a way of thinking about how employees' jobs can affect their well-being. (Later in the chapter the same model was used to show how job loss and underemployment can result in anguish.)

The third section focused extensively on work–family conflict. Given the importance of this area to both employees and organizations, a substantial amount of space was devoted to discussing it. In particular, we defined work–family conflict and enrichment, presented a conceptual model demonstrating how work and family interact with each other and related variables, and emphasized the various struggles faced by people who are working and nurturing a family at the same time. We then discussed the benefits that some organizations currently provide employees to help them deal with this conflict—benefits such as family-leave policies, child care, and elder care. Because more and more married people are dual-earner couples, we also considered some of the issues that make this situation stressful and explained how companies can help reduce the stress associated with juggling multiple careers and family responsibilities. Throughout this section, specific companies' work–life supports were highlighted to provide a sense of the many family-friendly benefits and services being offered to help reduce employees' stress.

The last two sections took a darker turn. First, we explored the psychological effects of job loss and underemployment in light of the increased number of layoffs at major U.S. corporations and the perceived threat of being laid off experienced by so many employees in the 21st century. Then we looked at some incredible statistics indicating the rise of workplace violence. In this context, employees at risk of becoming perpetrators were profiled, some recent research was reviewed, and a discussion was presented of two recent theoretical works that attempt to model the process through which workplace aggression and violence occur.

TEACHING THE CHAPTER

Because students are beginning to prepare to embark on their professional careers, this chapter discusses several complex and relevant concerns. The first portion of the chapter deals with a topic that is very familiar to college students—stress. However, the chapter will provide students with a theoretical framework for understanding this well-known concept along with research that is likely new to them. In addition to introducing students to stress-related theory and research, this chapter also discusses various coping strategies and techniques to alleviate stress. The accompanying exercises are meant to help students consider how the stress in their lives will likely change as they transition from college to the world of work and as they create their own families. Students also should have the opportunity to discuss various coping strategies that they have used, how their own strategies fit with the ones described in the chapter, and how this knowledge can be applied in the future.

The next section of the chapter discusses the sensitive issues of job loss and underemployment, which is particularly relevant given the recent economic downturn. This is clearly an especially important topic, as we have seen tremendous job losses through layoffs, downsizing, and bankruptcies. Unfortunately, many of us are likely to experience job loss at some point during our career. Class discussion may focus on how job loss affects internal and external perceptions of organizations with regard to financial health, competitive advantage, and organizational trust. You may want to consider comparing case studies of organizations that have been adversely affected by mass layoffs versus organizations that have been able to maintain their competitive advantage year after year.

This chapter concludes with a complex and highly emotional topic—workplace violence. Every year, horrendous acts of workplace violence are in the headlines. While the Department of Labor and Statistics suggests that about 5% of businesses experience workplace violence each year, few are prepared (Peek-Asa et al., 2007, found that less than 8% of hospitals have workplace violence preparedness programs; rates are probably lower for most other sectors). Class discussion may revolve around the handling of such situations. For example, how would you help a company move forward in the wake of a traumatic event such as a workplace shooting? The chapter also discusses research on aggression in the workplace, which may not be as headline-grabbing as shootings but is more typical in organizations.

SUGGESTED EXERCISES AND ASSIGNMENTS

Removing Stressors for a Day

Purpose The objective of this exercise is to have students figure out how to eliminate activities they engage in that contribute to stress.

Instructions During the class prior to this activity, ask students to list three discretionary activities they engage in regularly that they believe contribute to their stress levels. Examples of stressful activities they might discuss could include the following:

- Talking with a friend who is always having a crisis
- Taking on too many volunteer activities
- Spending too much time on the Internet
- Procrastinating on schoolwork
- Getting into arguments about unimportant topics

Ask students to spend a day or two avoiding these stressful activities. For example, if a student is always getting into intense discussions on Facebook, suggest that the student avoid doing so for a couple of days.

Discussion Questions

- How difficult was it to avoid these activities?
- Why do you think you engage in these activities? Is it out of force of habit? Boredom?
- What are some other behaviors you engage in that contribute to your stress levels? How could you avoid these activities?
- Is it always helpful to avoid stressful activities? What are some negative consequences of doing so?

Get the Stress Out!

Purpose The objective of this exercise is to have students consider how they cope with daily stress and what they can do to improve their coping strategies.

Instructions

- Ask students to make a list of the five biggest stressors they are facing right now, the five biggest stressors they faced 10 years ago, and what they believe will be their five biggest stressors 10 years from now. For each list, have the students identify coping strategies they use, used, and might use to mitigate the stressors. Tell them that they can use the text to help them identify coping strategies to be used in the future.
- Divide the class into groups of four to six.
- Have students discuss their lists and then create a master group list of the five biggest stressors of the present, past, and future. For each stressor, have students identify the coping strategies they use, used, and might use and how effective they believe those strategies are, were, and will be.
- If technology is available in the classroom, have students look at websites that deal with stress management. Then ask them to develop ways to improve their current stress management and think about how they might manage stress in the future. (There are many websites listed at the end of the chapter that might be useful for this exercise.)
- Groups should outline their findings in the following manner to share with the class:
  - Top five stressors: past, present, and future
  - Popular coping strategies: past and present only
  - Plans for stress management: present and future only

Discussion Questions

- How have your perceptions of stressful events changed throughout your life?
- Were these changes similar among your group members?
- How do you think your stress will change in the future?

Critical Incident for the Vice President of Human Resources

Purpose The objective of this exercise is to have students think about the complexities of ambiguous organizational situations.

Instructions

- *Prior to class:* You might want to copy the text below into a document that students can use during class. It is a brief description of a case that they can discuss and consider.

You are the vice president of human resources for a large Midwestern automaker that has fallen on tough economic times. Over the last 12 months, to keep your operation running, you have implemented a hiring freeze, eliminated all bonuses, and begun laying off employees. The labor union that represents your line employees has become increasingly hostile due to these changes, which does not help your already adversarial relationship with it. At this point, your margin for operating error is slim because your current contracts are the only thing keeping your company from falling into bankruptcy.

Last week a worker who was recently laid off arrived at the manufacturing plant, stormed into the main office, and demanded to see the management team responsible for laying him off. Before security could arrive on the scene, he opened fire with a shotgun, killing an administrative assistant, a foreman, and six line workers. In the end, he also took his own life.

- Ask students to develop an action plan to respond to this situation. For help, they can go to the websites on workplace violence listed at the end of the chapter. Ask them to address the following questions in their plans:
  - How would you handle notifying medical personnel, the victims' families, the news media, customers, employees, and the union?
  - Given the circumstances, should you close down the plant? If so, for how long? What would guide your decision?
  - What can you do to assist surviving employees?
  - How do you continue to meet customer obligations on such a slim budget and margin?
  - What policies and/or procedures could you put into place that might help prevent a similar incident? Is there anything in the selection process that could have screened out this individual?
  - How do you handle your own stress (as vice president of human resources) given the added pressure you are now experiencing?

Discussion Questions

- Have you ever encountered aggressive behavior in the workplace? What happened?
- What actions do you believe the organization could have taken prior to the incident to help decrease stress and increase communication between employees and management?
- What, as a coworker, would you do if you heard someone making threats about bringing a gun to work?
- Do you think smaller acts of aggression (e.g., throwing a stapler) are problematic in the workplace? What would you do about them if you were a coworker? A manager?

Reframing Activity

Purpose One easy way to address workplace stress is to reframe situations. This activity provides students with a demonstration of how they can view situations differently and in a more positive light.

Instructions You might want to copy the list below or develop some additional scenarios for students to consider. Present each situation, and ask students to come up with another way for the character to think of the situation that will make it seem less intimidating. You could also ask students to suggest ways that the individual can proactively cope with the scenario.

- Melissa, a social worker who has only been at her job for a year, has just been asked to step into a management position. She is much younger than any of the other managers, and she is worried that she does not have enough experience to perform the job effectively.
- Kendra is presenting her project proposal to her team. Typically, her presentations get a positive response, but one of her colleagues, Dean, seems irritated by her presentation. Afterward, Dean says to Kendra, "I know you mean well, but you obviously don't understand anything. This plan will be a disaster for our team!" Kendra feels like Dean does not respect her work or her position on the team and is considering asking to be transferred to a different team.
- Ricardo worked all night on a project to complete it by the deadline for a particularly difficult client. Ricardo is proud of his work, but neither his boss nor his client thanks him for his extra effort. As a result, he feels like he is unappreciated and is considering leaving his position.
- Benton has been trying to get in touch with a colleague, Layla, about a project they are supposed to work on. He has sent her several e-mails and voice mails. He knows she is in the office today, and he is still waiting to hear back from her. He feels as if she is a particularly irresponsible and disrespectful coworker.

Discussion Questions
- In these scenarios, are the characters making some assumptions? What are some examples?
- In these scenarios, the characters seem to think that they are unable to deal effectively with the stressor. Do you believe these are reasonable perspectives? Why or why not?
- What are some different ways these characters can deal with the problem? Why might these alternative approaches be more effective?

Worker Stress and Well-Being in the Movies

Purpose A number of movies include themes that directly apply to the concepts discussed in this chapter—job stress, work–family conflict, job loss, and workplace conflict/violence. This activity will give students the opportunity to see the class material come to life and to discuss the issues in specific detail.

Instructions Screen one or more of the following movies in class or assign them for homework. Follow up with a class discussion. Alternatively, you could show segments of the movies during class lectures to illustrate concepts. This list is by no means exhaustive.
- Work–family conflict/roles
  - *Mr. Mom* (1983): Starring Michael Keaton, who trades in his career to take over home responsibilities so that his wife can pursue her career goals.

- *Baby Boom* (1987): Starring Diane Keaton, who plays a high-powered ad executive who is working her way to the top of a male-dominated corporate hierarchy when the will of a recently departed cousin names her guardian of a 13-month-old baby girl.
- *One Fine Day* (1996): Starring Michelle Pfeiffer and George Clooney as single parents trying to juggle their career demands with caring for their young children.
- *Raising Helen* (2004): Starring Kate Hudson as a young, career-oriented woman who unexpectedly becomes the guardian of her sister's three young children, which derails her own career ambitions.
- *Brats* (2004): A documentary examining how children in military families grow up differently from their peers due to the demands of their parents' jobs.
- *Waitress* (2009): A waitress becomes motivated by an unexpected pregnancy to save money and escape her overbearing husband by baking pies.
- *Mad Men* (TV series from 2007−2015): This series, which dramatizes the turbulent life of an ad agency and its employees through the 1960s and into the 1970s, is filled with themes ranging from sexism, racism, work−family conflict, workplace stress, supervisor−subordinate conflicts, etc.
- *I Don't Know How She Does It* (2011): Starring Sarah Jessica Parker in a comedy about her attempts to juggle being a finance executive with a husband and two children.
- *Steve Jobs* (2015): Amid the story of an ambitious entrepreneur who reshaped personal computers and communication are some interesting insights into the work−life balance (and imbalance).
- Work/job stress
  - *Falling Down* (1993): Starring Michael Douglas, who is having one of the worst days a person can have. This entertaining, yet disturbing, movie examines work pressures and family pressures as well as how mounting stress can push a person over the edge.
  - *The Devil Wears Prada* (2002): Starring Anne Hathaway, who plays a stressed-out assistant to a fashion magazine editor (as performed by Meryl Streep) who is overly demanding and controlling.
  - *North Country* (2005): Starring Charlize Theron, who deals with many stressors (including sexual harassment) as a woman working in a coal mine.
  - *Morning Glory* (2010): Rachel McAdams plays Becky, a recently fired TV producer who must deal with sexist cohosts, hiring new reporters, and other hassles in order to save a failing morning show.
  - *Murder by Proxy* (2012): This documentary traces the etymology of the term "going postal" by investigating workplace violence, including a 1991 mass shooting in a post office.
  - *The Intern* (2015): This comedy starring Anne Hathaway and Robert De Niro touches on issues involving career development and work−life stress.
- Job loss
  - *Roger & Me* (1989): A documentary by Michael Moore chronicling General Motors plant closings in Flint, Michigan, and the resulting effects of job loss on the town and GM employees.

- *Glengarry Glen Ross* (1992): Real estate salesmen are faced with job loss and a decision that will either make or break them.
- *Office Space* (1999): The classic I/O film depicting employees who are downtrodden in their jobs and the measures they take when consultants are brought in to implement downsizing.
- *Fun with Dick and Jane* (2005): Starring Jim Carrey as an executive who unexpectedly loses his job and makes numerous attempts at crime to maintain his lifestyle.
- *The Pursuit of Happyness* (2006): Will Smith stars as a father who receives a chance to save himself and his son from homelessness through an unpaid internship at a prestigious brokerage firm.
- *Up in the Air* (2009): Starring George Clooney as a consultant hired by downsizing companies to fire people and present them with their severance options.
- *The Internship* (2013): Starring Owen Wilson and Vince Vaughn as salesmen who lose their jobs and are forced to take internships at a tech company, where their skills and past experience don't fit.
- Workplace conflict
  - *American Dream* (1992): A documentary by Barbara Kopple that depicts the six-year labor dispute at a meat-packing plant in Minnesota.
  - *Employee of the Month* (2006): Starring Dane Cook as an otherwise lazy employee who engages in a heated competition with a coworker to become employee of the month.
  - *The Promotion* (2008): Seann William Scott stars as a supermarket assistant manager who has to decide how to behave toward a rival for a promotion he desperately wants.
  - *Horrible Bosses* (2011) or *Horrible Bosses 2* (2014): This comedy series illustrates (and exaggerates) several dysfunctional member–leader relationships and the potential consequences.

Discussion Questions

- What were the major themes depicted in these movies?
- Did the characters meet the demands they faced? Were their coping strategies effective? What other coping strategies could they have used?
- Do you believe these are accurate portrayal of stress/conflict/job loss?
- How were others affected by the main characters' situations in the movie?

EVALUATING "TAKING IT TO THE FIELD"

The Chapter 11 activity involves Michael Yurttas of the Dutler Accountancy Firm, who is concerned about satisfying working mothers despite needing them to work 60–70 hours a week for two months of the year. Students may have a variety of suggestions for Michael; below are some guidelines for evaluating their responses.

Poor responses...	▪ Fail to provide concrete solutions for Michael.
	▪ Argue that focusing on retaining women at the organization is unimportant.
	▪ Suggest any illegal approaches (e.g., hiring only unmarried women or women without children).
Good responses...	▪ Acknowledge the importance of retaining female workers.
	▪ Provide concrete and helpful suggestions, such as providing onsite day care and offering other incentives (such as providing telecommuting or flextime during other times of the year).
Excellent responses...	▪ Acknowledge the importance of retaining women in the company.
	▪ Note the point that sometimes work is slow, and leverage that point in the recommendations (e.g., offering reduced hours during the summer, asking women who have left the company whether they would be willing to come in part time during the busy season to help other employees).
	▪ Identify additional approaches or policies that might make the work easier and more enjoyable for everyone, not just working mothers. For example, students might suggest changing incentives, since other workers might not be interested only in overtime pay as a reward. Students might also suggest some of the work arrangements suggested in the text, including telecommuting, paid sabbaticals, and child-care benefits.

EVALUATING "APPLICATION QUESTIONS"

1. Consider a recent stressful event you experienced at work. What types of job-related, emotional, and physiological strains did you experience as a result of this event? What are some problem-focused and emotion-focused coping strategies you might have used? What could the organization have done to help you deal with this stress?

   Evaluation Guide: Because this question relates to student experiences, responses will vary. However, the following guidelines will help ensure that students are answering the questions appropriately and understand concepts appropriately:

   ▪ Job-related strains encompass responses such as "I don't feel like working hard" or "I call in sick to work more, even when I'm not sick."

   ▪ Emotional strains encompass responses such as "I feel angry or sad at work."

   ▪ Physiological strains encompass responses such as "I have headaches and stomach aches" or "I get sick more often."

- In terms of coping strategies, students should clearly recognize the difference between problem-focused and emotion-focused coping. For example, a student who felt disrespected by his or her boss and therefore had a frank discussion with the boss about the situation would be engaged in problem-focused coping. Alternatively, a student who went for a run after work to blow off steam would be engaged in emotion-focused coping.
- Depending upon the situation the student identifies as stressful, the organization may have been able to offer support, including changes in job expectations, training, better leadership, appreciation for services rendered, or more control over his or her work.

2. Telecommuting is becoming more popular in a number of different companies. Consider your own schoolwork and how productive you are when you are working at home or in your dorm room, compared to when you are in a computer lab or a library. What are some benefits you have found to working at home? What are some difficulties? If you've taken an online course, how does that environment compare to a traditional classroom setting? What changes have you needed to make to your work habits to ensure you finish your online class successfully?

Evaluation Guide: This question allows students to consider their own current work habits and what is best for them. If students have difficulty coming up with responses, you could consider the following points:

- Students may encounter different distractions in different environments. For example, when working at home or in their dorm room, they may get distracted by the Internet, friends stopping by to visit, pets, children, phone calls, and a number of other interruptions. They may also lose access to helpful resources that are available at the library or elsewhere on campus (including tangibles such as books and articles as well as advice and support from fellow students). Alternatively, they may benefit from working at home by having a more comfortable chair or desk area, a quieter work environment, or more freedom about when to take breaks.
- Many students might immediately indicate that they would prefer to work from home all the time. It can be helpful to ask them whether it would be difficult for them to set scheduled work times, to find opportunities to socialize with other people, and to prevent work and leisure time from bleeding into each other. Discussing this may also help students to consider how to change their own work habits to avoid wasting time by studying in front of the TV and similar types of behaviors.
- For students who have little workplace experience, it can also help to compare online classes to traditional classes. Many students are shocked by how much more carefully they need to plan and schedule their time, and how disciplined they need to be to avoid social media and other distractions while working on class content. This exercise can provide a helpful discussion about how those habits they need to build might also make them more effective in traditional classrooms or in the workplace.

3. If you were to take a new job right now, what types of benefits would be most appealing to you? How might those benefits help you avoid common stressors such as work–family conflict, healthcare concerns, and job demands? Do you think you would find the same benefits helpful five years from now? Why or why not?

Evaluation Guide: Responses will likely vary greatly depending upon the age and prior work experience of your population of students. However, the following might be common answers:

- Younger, traditional students will likely be more interested in issues related to education, loan repayment, fitness, flextime, and time off. Many of these students are also enthralled by convenience benefits such as on-campus salons, dry cleaning, and "fun" aspects like pool tables or videogames. However, as they think about their futures, some will be more interested in family-friendly benefits, such as daycares, maternity/paternity leave, or adoption support.

- Older, nontraditional students who have more workplace experience tend to be less impressed by convenience benefits. Instead, they tend to be more interested in practical issues such as healthcare and health screenings, flexible work arrangements, and child-care or education assistance. Within the next five years, some of these individuals may become part of the "sandwich generation," where they are responsible both for their children and for their aging parents, so elder-care support may become more relevant to them.

- Encourage students to think about how they might address their changing needs for different benefits. Does this mean they will have to renegotiate their employment terms with the organization? Or will they need to seek out new jobs in order to obtain these benefits?

4. Underemployment is a common problem in the U.S. Think of a time when you were stuck in a job or a class that was too easy and failed to challenge you. What were some frustrations with that situation? Do you think these frustrations would become more or less intense the longer you were in that situation? Did you take any steps to try to add challenge to that experience, and if so, what were they?

Evaluation Guide: Sometimes, students believe that having an easy or mindless job will be relaxing or fun, but often, this lack of challenge leads to boredom and stress. Students who have been bored for long periods of time might be able to relate the feeling of endlessness and unproductivity. Students may have good suggestions for how to improve this, such as job crafting, engaging with coworkers, and reading relevant books to help develop their skills. However, there might also be some suggestions that are not effective, such as surfing the web, reading off-topic books, and the like.

5. Imagine that a friend was recently laid off. He has only been unemployed for a few weeks, but already he is feeling depressed and hopeless about finding another job. What might you do to help him? What advice would you offer him?

Evaluation Guide: As noted in the text, there is a fair amount of research on unemployment and stress. Some potential discussion points include the following:

- Your friend may benefit from adding additional structure to his day. For example, he should set aside specific times to conduct his job search as well as to engage in some stress-relieving activities such as exercising, spending time with friends, and so on.
- Finding opportunities to receive social support may also help. For example, joining a job search group would bring him into contact with people who have similar problems who can listen and suggest solutions. The more he can stop thinking about the job loss and start thinking about a new opportunity, the lower his stress will be.
- Your friend can also find a number of ways to engage in problem-focused and emotion-focused coping. For example, if he feels that he does not have the skills necessary to be employable, he could take some classes or practice his skills to increase his confidence. Additionally, he could make sure to spend some time doing enjoyable activities during the day to help him feel better so that he can continue to focus on his job search.

HIGHLIGHTED STUDY FOR DISCUSSION

Shimazu, A., Shaufeli, W. B., & Taris, T. W. (2010). How does workaholism affect worker health and performance? The mediating role of coping. *International Journal of Behavioral Medicine, 17,* 154–160.

In this article, the authors define workaholism and examine whether it has deleterious effects on worker health and performance. Short and straightforward, it can serve as a helpful introduction to structural equation modeling (SEM) for students who are not familiar with the technique. The main points of the article are as follows:

- Previous studies had established a negative relationship between workaholism and health. This study examined whether coping skills mediate the relationship between workaholism and health as well as between workaholism and performance.
- Participants in the study were employees of a construction machinery company in Japan. You could discuss with students whether this population might differ from others (given that Japan tends to have longer workweeks and a stronger work ethic compared to many other countries).
- The authors assessed workaholism, active coping (analyzing information to solve problems), emotional discharge (taking out frustrations on others), psychological distress, physical complaints, and self-rated job performance. It could be helpful to discuss the problem with having the job incumbent provide ratings on all of these scales, particularly the job performance scale.
- The results indicated that workaholism had a strong direct link with ill health (.63). It also had indirect links, such that workaholism led to more active

coping, which led to ill health. Workaholism also led to more emotional discharge, which led to more ill health. Meanwhile, workaholism was not directly related to higher performance; it was, however, indirectly related through active coping. Many of these findings would be fruitful topics for discussion—for example, why workaholism is not directly related to performance.

■ In sum, workaholics spent more time thinking about problems they were facing and dealing with their emotions through other people, tendencies that had mixed results: Active coping led to higher levels of performance and ill health. Emotional discharge was related to ill health but appeared to be unrelated to performance. The authors suggest that if organizations want to ensure healthy employees, they should attempt to reduce workaholism among them.

WEB LEARNING

Title	Address
National Institute for Occupational Safety and Health (NIOSH): Stress at Work	http://www.cdc.gov/niosh/topics/stress
Stress management resources from Mind Tools	http://www.mindtools.com/smpage.html
How Stuff Works: Stress Management Center	http://health.howstuffworks.com/wellness/stress-management
Work and Family Researchers Network: Resources for Workplace Practice	https://workfamily.sas.upenn.edu/static/index_business
U.S. Department of Labor: Economy at a Glance (includes unemployment numbers)	http://www.bls.gov/eag/eag.us.htm
U.S. Department of Labor, OSHA: Workplace Violence	https://www.osha.gov/SLTC/workplaceviolence/
NIOSH Risk Factors and Prevention Strategies: Violence in the Workplace	http://www.cdc.gov/niosh/docs/96-100/
The National Institute for the Prevention of Workplace Violence	http://www.workplaceviolence911.com
U.S. Department of Health and Human Services: Eldercare Locator	http://www.eldercare.gov/Eldercare.NET/Public/Index.aspx
Fortune 100 Best Companies to Work For	http://fortune.com/best-companies/?iid=sr-link1
The Riley Guide: Coping with Job Loss	http://www.rileyguide.com/cope.html

Group Processes and Work Teams

Chapter Summary

This chapter introduced the concepts of work groups and work teams and discussed the processes involved in the use of such groups in organizations. The chapter began with a definition of work groups and a review of group processes. It then discussed social influence in groups in the context of norms, roles, conflict, cohesion, and social loafing, applying those elements to organizational functioning. Tuckman's model of group development and the popular punctuated equilibrium model, as well as theories that seek to combine these models were then presented.

Group decision making was another area emphasized in this chapter. Because groups are entrusted with important organizational decisions, considerable time was spent discussing a process that, when followed, is likely to result in effective decision making. This five-step process emphasizes the quality of the social interaction among group members—an issue that was discussed in connection with some of the common mistakes made at certain points in the process. This topic led logically to ineffective decision making, with a particular emphasis on groupthink. Here the chapter presented historical examples of groupthink and discussed its antecedents and symptoms in light of organizational situations.

The last section focused on work teams, which have become incredibly popular in modern-day organizations. The chapter discussed various types of work teams and gave examples of each, placing particular emphasis on self-managed work teams both because of their prevalence in organizations and because of their inherent complexities. A few examples of organizations currently using work teams were provided, the idea of shared mental models was introduced, and the determinants of work-team effectiveness were identified. The chapter concluded with a discussion of current trends, including virtual teams and multiteam systems.

TEACHING THE CHAPTER

Almost all students will have had some experience with teams—likely from involvement with athletic, academic-related, or community organizations. If students have not had these experiences, they may relate to teams they have seen on TV or observed in their own family life. Therefore, the subject matter in this chapter should come easily to students, and a great deal of discussion should emerge based on their experiences. The only potential "sticking point" that students may have is differentiating between *groups* and *teams*, terms that are used interchangeably in the text and that are even confused a great deal in the team/group literature.

The exercises below are designed to help students consider issues regarding groups in a variety of situations. The first exercise draws on students' experience with teams and encourages them to consider and analyze what makes a team successful or unsuccessful. The next exercise simulates a self-managed work-team environment and introduces some team competition to reinforce the chapter material on team development and decision making. The third exercise focuses on groupthink, offering students a glimpse of this concept in action.

Many team-building exercises and activities are available online and in other publications, and you may find these to be valuable sources for reinforcing the concepts in the chapter. An exercise that has been well received in classes and training seminars is the "lost in the desert/mountains/ocean/arctic" exercise, which involves comparing individual judgment/processing with that of a group. Another interesting topic for students to discuss is the future of organizational teams and the use of virtual teams. One of the Internet website links provided at the end of this chapter focuses on research and practice regarding virtual teams. Addressing the pros and cons associated with the use of virtual teams in organizations, as well as how technology may impact students' future teamwork in their careers, should stimulate lively class discussion.

SUGGESTED EXERCISES AND ASSIGNMENTS

The Group That Sticks Together . . .

Purpose Students will discuss effective and ineffective teams and the role that cohesiveness plays in team success.

Instructions

- After presenting the chapter material related to group cohesion, divide the class into groups of four to six.
- *Exercise Option 1:* Ask each group to focus on one of the categories of teams listed below:
  - Business (famous management teams)
  - Athletics (professional, collegiate)
  - Entertainment (television or movies)
  - A personal experience
- *Exercise Option 2:* In class, show an episode of a reality TV show that involves teamwork. Examples of shows that have worked well in class include scenes from *The Apprentice, Survivor,* and *Real World/Road Rules Challenge.*
- After either exercise option, have students discuss the following questions in their groups and then prepare a brief report to present to the class.
  - Why was your team effective?
  - Could it have been more effective? Did the team encounter any problems? If so, how were they handled?
  - To what extent did the group communicate? Did communication flow freely in the group? Why or why not?
  - How did the group make decisions?
  - Were there social loafers in these groups?
  - Did any symptoms of groupthink emerge?

Discussion Questions

- What elements are common to successful teams? To unsuccessful teams?
- What, if any, common problems did these teams encounter?
- Do you notice any differences in the communication patterns of cohesive and noncohesive groups?

Rope Square

Purpose In this exercise, students must communicate clearly and efficiently with their fellow group members to accomplish a task.

Instructions

- This activity is best for about 12 or fewer people. If your group is larger than this, consider breaking them into several groups or having some students serve as observers. Make sure you have a safe, open place to play the game (e.g., go outside, or move desks and chairs to the edges of the room).

- Ask students to volunteer to be team members. Let them know that they will be blindfolded for this activity, and allow anyone who would find this unpleasant to opt out. Those who opt out can be supervisors of the activity (see below).
- Ask students to spread out in the room, put their blindfolds in place, and spin around a few times to become disoriented.
- Provide one of the students with a length of rope or string (about 10 yards long). Tell them they must form this rope into a perfect square by working together.
- Supervise the activity (or assign a student to each group to supervise) so that nobody runs into anything or gets hurt. You may also choose to intervene if students become frustrated.
- When students have had about 30 minutes to perform the task, ask them to remove their blindfolds and come together as a group.

Discussion Questions
- How well did you do at the task?
- What prevented you from accomplishing the task quickly? What frustrated you?
- What seemed to work well?
- How does this relate to completing group work, especially in a workplace where some of your colleagues might be working remotely?

Flying the Friendly Skies

Purpose Students will engage in a group exercise that illustrates the steps of team development, as discussed in the text.

Instructions
- *Prior to class:* You will need the following supplies for each group:
  - Sheets of blank paper (with each group receiving the same number of sheets of paper)
  - Measuring tape
  - Markers
  - Scissors
  - *Optional:* You may also consider giving the winning team a prize.
- After presenting Tuckman's five stages of team development (forming, storming, norming, performing, and adjourning), divide the class into groups of four to six students. To the extent possible, place students in groups with other students they may not know very well.
- Each group must assign one member to serve as the observer/recorder. This member will report the behavior and activities of the group, as well as classify behaviors into one of Tuckman's five stages.
- The group task is to make quality paper airplanes.

- Explain the criteria for successful performance (and announce a prize to the winning team, if applicable). Successful performance is based on the following criteria:
  - *Quantity:* number of airplanes assembled
  - *Quality:* length of flight, design, appearance
- You might want to suggest that each team designate roles to its members (e.g., research and development, assembly, test piloting, decoration design, etc.). Teams may also want to develop an action plan before proceeding with the task and spend time developing a prototype before beginning to assemble airplanes.
- Set a time limit (10 minutes or longer) for the groups to assemble as many airplanes as possible.
- After the time limit has expired, have the observer count the number of assembled airplanes and select the plane to be used in a flight test.
- One representative from each group should explain the design of the plane as well as the meaning behind any decorations on the plane. He or she will also launch the plane to assess its flight performance (this is where a measuring tape comes in handy).
- Select a winning group based on flight length, decoration, and number of planes produced.
- Have observers (and team members) discuss the extent to which their teams moved through Tuckman's five stages.

Discussion Questions
- To what extent did your team follow Tuckman's model? If the team did not follow this model closely, why do you think this happened?
- What problems did your team encounter during this exercise?
- What was the toughest part of this task?
- Do you think your teamwork affected the measures of team performance (quantity/quality of airplanes)? Why or why not?

Culture Shock Activity

Purpose The objective of this exercise is to give students a simulated experience of working to accomplish a task in a group with a different culture.

Instructions
- This activity is best for smaller classes (20–30 students) and can take up to an hour. However, most students find it to be a fun experience.
- Divide the class into two groups, and place the groups in separate rooms. Each group of students will be from a different culture. The following are suggestions for how each group might behave, but you can replace any rules with different ones that you think would be interesting.
  - Group X culture
  - This is a very friendly and warm culture. Members like to stand close to one another, and they touch elbows when they greet each other.

- Members are also very polite; before they get down to business, they ask one another about what is going on—how everyone is doing, what everyone has been up to.
- Females are in charge. The oldest female is the leader, and other members of the group show respect for her by shaking their heads back and forth (in a "no" motion") whenever they address her.
- Whenever a cultural rule is violated, the nearest person says, "Eep eep!" and walks over to the female leader.
- Group Y culture
- This is a more reserved culture. Members like to have a lot of space between them and other people, and they tug their own ear to greet another person.
- Members also like to get down to business. Asking others about themselves only takes place after business has been discussed.
- Males are in charge. The male with the shortest hair is the leader, and other members show respect by rubbing their own stomach when the leader approaches them.
- Whenever a cultural rule is violated, the leader claps his hands, and all members of the group move away from the person who violated the rule.
- Allow each group a little time to practice these cultural rules among themselves. Inform each group that their task is to determine whether they think they would like to partner with the other culture to form a new technology firm. Send students (in pairs or trios, depending upon the size of your class) to visit the other culture and learn about it. Allow students a couple of minutes to visit the group, and then ask them to return to their original group to share their findings. You may repeat this step as many times as you like with new visitors, potentially until everyone has visited the opposite culture.

Discussion Questions

- Do you think you would want to work with this other culture? Why or why not?
- What do you think are some of the rules in the other culture? What are the actual rules in that culture?
- What could members of Group X/Group Y do to help make working with the other culture easier?
- What might be some potential trouble areas between the two groups?

Groupthink Prevention Strategies

Purpose The objective of this exercise is to have students think about the occurrence of groupthink and how to prevent it.

Instructions

- After you have presented the material on groupthink, divide the class into groups of four to six students.
- Have teams assign each group member to one of the following roles:
  - Strong, biased leader

- Mindguard
- Devil's advocate
- Observer who records the social behavior in the discussion (this person does not participate in the discussion)
- *Optional role:* Followers who support the leader's position
- In their groups, students should discuss an issue that has recently been in the news. The group must decide on a specific course of action. Once you have given groups sufficient discussion time, ask them to report their decision (if reached). Also, solicit the observer's comments on the decision-making process that occurred in the group as well as any symptoms or consequences of groupthink that may have surfaced.

Discussion Questions
- How difficult was it to maintain the role you were assigned?
- Do you think governmental decision makers face groupthink?
- Do you think groupthink can be eliminated or minimized?

EVALUATING "TAKING IT TO THE FIELD"

The activity for Chapter 12 involves a question from Siran Belekdanian at WeldCo, where service people and salespeople have differing viewpoints on how the work should be done. The salespeople are focused on making sales in any way possible, even when it means making promises the service people cannot keep. The service people, meanwhile, are purposely slowing down work to get back at the salespeople. The prompt asks students to think of three suggestions for Siran. Below are some suggestions for evaluating responses.

Poor responses...	■ Provide superficial responses to Siran—for example, suggesting team barbecues or team-building activities without addressing the root problem.
	■ Provide fewer than three suggestions.
	■ Fail to include members of both teams in devising a solution.
	■ Side with only one group (salespeople or service people).
Good responses...	■ Identify or speculate about some of the root causes of the mismatch (e.g., salespeople trying to meet unreasonable goals, the service department being understaffed).
	■ Suggest that Siran bring together both teams to discuss the issue and find solutions together.
	■ Discuss *one* of the following issues:
	■ Inappropriate group norms (e.g., selling more than they can deliver).
	■ Roles (e.g., whether any team members have a responsibility to check in with the other team).

- Cohesion (e.g., finding ways to build better and routine connections between members of each team).
- Conflict (e.g., discussing that there is likely a lot of task conflict and/or process conflict; students should discuss that allowing employees to share their unique experiences and perspectives can help others to understand how their actions affect the other department).
- Groupthink (e.g., if the teams are too insular, they may not see how some of their decisions, such as slowing down service, are harmful).
- Tuckman's stages of group development (e.g., the teams appear to be in the storming phase and may need to develop clear overall norms to feel more unity).
- Social loafing (e.g., ensuring that salespeople who oversell are held responsible for doing so; ensuring that service people who are slowing down service are held accountable).
- Suggest ways that Siran might apply the five steps of good group decision making (found in Table 12.2 in the book) to the issue.

Excellent responses...
- Identify or speculate about some of the root causes of the mismatch (e.g., salespeople trying to meet unreasonable goals, the service department being understaffed).
- Suggest that Siran bring together both teams to discuss the issue and find solutions together.
- Discuss *two or more* of the following issues:
  - Inappropriate group norms (e.g., selling more than they can deliver).
  - Roles (e.g., whether any team members have a responsibility to check in with the other team).
  - Cohesion (e.g., finding ways to build better and routine connections between members of each team).
  - Conflict (e.g., discussing that there is likely a lot of task conflict and/or process conflict; students should discuss that allowing employees to share their unique experiences and perspectives can help others to understand how their actions affect the other department).
  - Groupthink (e.g., if the teams are too insular, they may not see how some of their decisions, such as slowing down service, are harmful).
  - Tuckman's stages of group development (e.g., the teams appear to be in the storming phase and may need to develop clear overall norms to feel more unity).

- Social loafing (e.g., ensuring that salespeople who oversell are held responsible for doing so; ensuring that service people who are slowing down service are held accountable).
- Whether the teams have a solid mental model of how work is done. Students may also suggest cross-training, or having people from the two departments swap for a day to experience some of the problems they face.
- Suggest ways that Siran might apply the five steps of good group decision making (found in Table 12.2 in the book) to the issue.

EVALUATING "APPLICATION QUESTIONS"

1. What is an example of a group you've been a part of that was highly cohesive. What made it that way? How could some of those qualities be instilled in a workplace team?

   Evaluation Guide: Students will likely come up with a variety of suggestions for this question. The following are common suggestions:
   - If students have difficulty thinking of groups, you could prompt them to think of social groups (hobby clubs, fraternities/sororities, honor societies).
   - Prompt students to think of what sorts of experiences and activities make them feel close to other group members. For example, fraternity/sorority members might be able to discuss the difficult tasks pledges had to accomplish; honor society members might talk about how hard they had to work to be admitted.
   - Discuss with students why having groups face common challenges and difficulties can help people feel more connected (e.g., they know they have all been through the same things; being in a group that is hard to get into makes people appreciate being a part of the group).

2. Consider a time when you experienced social loafing in a group (in a class or at work). What were some aspects of the situation that caused social loafing to occur? What could your instructor or boss have done to decrease social loafing?

   Evaluation Guide:
   - For students who had to do a lot of the work in the group, ask them to explain why other group members did not work. Did they get to evaluate other group members' work? Was there a way for the instructor/employer to notice individual effort and skill? Were the other members uninterested in the reward (such as effective performance or a good project grade)?
   - For students who are brave enough to admit they have engaged in social loafing, ask why they chose to let someone else do the work—was it a purposeful decision? How did they feel after the fact? Would they have behaved differently if they knew they would have to work with the same group members again?

3. Consider a group that you are currently a part of. In your opinion, did you find that the group followed Tuckman's model as it developed, or did it follow the more oscillating style of punctuated equilibrium? Give some specific examples to support your opinion.

Evaluation Guide:

▪ Students may differ in whether they believe their experiences followed Tuckman's model versus the punctuated equilibrium model. Talk about differences in the students' examples. For instance, some students may discuss joining a group that was already formed; others might discuss being part of a newly-formed group. Some groups may be permeable, and constantly have new members; others might be firmly established, where new members are not accepted or invited. Highlight how some of these differences affect the phase a group might be in, and whether groups experienced the phases in order or not.

▪ Students who believe their group is in a "forming" stage might mention being on good behavior, trying to make a good impression, not being sure of how to do things the "right" way, and not being sure who to trust or distrust in the group.

▪ Students who believe their group is in the "storming" stage might mention the emergence of group members' personalities and group conflicts, a jostling for power or status within the group, conflict over jobs or tasks, and the emergence of more disagreement among members about how to do the work or how well to do the work.

▪ Students who believe their group is in the "norming" stage might mention being able to articulate some of the "rules" of the group (timeliness, what should be accomplished each time they meet) and finding close friends within the group who share their opinions.

▪ Students who believe their group is in the "performing" stage might mention that most of the conflict is worked out and that they are able to focus on tasks or goals.

▪ Students who believe their group is in the final stage, "adjourning," might mention finishing a project and dissolving the group, feeling that the group no longer shares a common goal, or feeling sad as the cohesion begins to disappear among group members. It may also be worth asking all students if they ever expect their groups to reach an adjourning stage and, if so, when it might occur.

4. Imagine you are working with a virtual group to put together a presentation on teamwork. How might you use technology to help you communicate, share ideas, and design your presentation slides? What parts of that experience do you think would be most difficult, and how might you overcome them?

Evaluation Guide:

▪ Students may rely heavily on technology they are familiar with (e.g., texts and e-mails). Encourage them to consider other methods of communication, such as teleconferences, virtual meeting rooms, virtual worlds such as Second Life, and other creative approaches. It may also help to encourage them to think about the tradeoffs between having synchronous communication (e.g., chat rooms) versus asynchronous communication (e.g., discussion boards where people may not be posting at the same time).

■ Many students may have had some experience in virtual groups and will understand some of the difficulties that come with them: finding time to get together, making sure communication is clear (e.g., crafting e-mail messages so that they do not sound unintentionally rude), and increased issues with social loafing. Help students connect general suggestions for cohesion and team building into the virtual world (e.g., the importance of sharing goals, having good communication and sharing among members, checking assumptions) and emphasize that in virtual groups, one must be even more careful to ensure everyone is on the same page.

■ Have students consider how group members can ensure that they stay on track. For example, on conference calls, it is easy for someone to ramble on and not be able to see that other members are becoming restless, so setting a timer and limiting how long any individual can speak may help prevent people from derailing the group. Likewise, assigning roles to group members, such as "devil's advocate," can help the group think critically about ideas without discomfort or conflict, even in a virtual team.

5. Consider a job you once had or a group project you worked on in a class. In order to work with others, you likely had a shared mental model. Give some examples of what might have been part of this mental model you shared with group members.

Evaluation Guide:

■ Students will have a variety of ideas about this question. Students who are thinking about a social group may think about how a group makes a decision (e.g., is one person typically responsible for driving? For making reservations?). Students who are thinking about a work situation may consider how workers can seamlessly take on one another's tasks (e.g., a student who works in a kitchen may be able to describe how cooks cover for one another during bathroom breaks or during the dinner rush).

■ If students have difficulty coming up with examples, you could prompt them by asking about cases where a mental model didn't exist and they were unable to anticipate what someone else was going to do. Ask them how they would go about helping others build a common mental model.

HIGHLIGHTED STUDY FOR DISCUSSION

Liden, R. C., Wayne, S. J., Jaworski, R. A., & Bennett, N. (2004). Social loafing: A field investigation. *Journal of Management, 30,* 285–300.

This article is an interesting example of moving from lab studies to field studies. It is somewhat long and uses some relatively complex statistical techniques (hierarchical linear modeling), but the method and techniques are clearly described and should be relatively accessible for most college students. It is also a nice example of the interesting questions that are generated when findings don't go as expected. Key points include the following:

- The authors provide evidence from lab-based student studies about social loafing in work groups. They argue that there is a need for more data on actual work groups, and they present these data in the article.
- Specifically, the authors hypothesize the following:
  Higher levels of task interdependence will be related to less social loafing.
  - Low task visibility will be related to more social loafing.
  - Work groups in which there is little sense of justice (distributive and/or procedural) will experience more social loafing.
  - Larger groups will experience more social loafing.
  - Highly cohesive groups will experience less social loafing.
  - Individuals who believe there is more social loafing will also engage in higher levels of social loafing.
- A total of 168 employees and 23 managers completed measures on the variables. Employees reported on task interdependence, task visibility, distributive justice, and procedural justice. Managers completed measures on group size, group cohesiveness, perceived coworker loafing, and social loafing for the participating employees.
- All of the hypotheses were supported by the data, with the exception of two. First, procedural justice was not related to social loafing. Second, individuals who believed their coworkers engaged in a great deal of social loafing actually engaged in less loafing themselves, contrary to what was predicted. It may be useful to discuss why students believe those two hypotheses were not supported. Were the authors justified in their original hypotheses? Why or why not?
- It may also be worthwhile to discuss one of the strengths of this article—that social loafing by individuals was rated by the manager instead of the employee. Discuss with students why this might have been an important thing to do in this study.

WEB LEARNING

Title	Address
Leading Virtually blog	http://www.leadingvirtually.com/
Fifth Generation Work—Virtual Organization: Links to information and articles about virtual teams	http://www.seanet.com/~daveg/articles.htm
University of Michigan: Research Center for Group Dynamics	http://www.rcgd.isr.umich.edu
NASA: Teams and Teamwork	http://www.hq.nasa.gov/office/hqlibrary/ppm/ppm5.htm
Center for Media and Democracy: Groupthink (includes recent news examples)	http://www.prwatch.org/search/node/groupthink
What Is Groupthink?	http://www.psysr.org/about/pubs_resources/groupthink%20overview.htm
Psychtests.com: Team Roles Test	http://testyourself.psychtests.com/testid/3113
List of research articles relevant to social loafing	http://kraut.hciresearch.org/recent-articles-and-chapters#Collab
Team-building activities for the classroom	http://thiagi.com/games.html http://www.teampedia.net/wiki/index.php?title=Main_Page http://www.ultimatecampresource.com/site/camp-activities/team-building-games-and-initiatives.page-1.html http://homepages.abdn.ac.uk/j.masthoff/pages/teaching/CS3021/practicals/MoonExercise.pdf http://scoutingweb.com/scoutingweb/subpages/survivalgame.htm

Leadership

Chapter Summary

This chapter provides an overview of leadership, with an emphasis on the theoretical and empirical work done in the field. The chapter began by defining leadership and demonstrating how the concept of power and its different types relate to leadership processes. It then emphasized that leaders use different types of power in different situations and that some leaders rely on some types of power more than other types.

Next, the major theories of leadership were presented, with an eye toward tracing their historical development; the rationale here was to show that history provides clues about how our thinking on leadership has evolved and become more sophisticated. The chapter then described trait theories as the first real systematic approach to leadership, explaining that because no traits consistently emerged as necessary to be a good leader, this approach was largely abandoned (albeit revived later) in favor of research on leadership behaviors. The latter has revealed that some effective leaders exhibit mostly consideration behaviors, whereas others exhibit mostly initiating-structure behaviors. Taking a different direction, the chapter then considered research on situational and individual moderators, as well as contingencies. In particular, Fiedler's theory was presented as an important new approach that eventually came under criticism—with the result that leadership advocates began looking elsewhere for a theoretical orientation. This section also addressed path–goal theory and leader–member exchange (LMX) theory.

In a later section, considerable time was spent discussing two contemporary theories—implicit leadership theory (ILT) and transformational leadership theory—that have great potential to help us understand leadership processes. It was also noted that the perspective on leadership taken by ILT and transformational leadership is very different from that of more traditional theories. The chapter also notes two approaches that are related to transformational leadership: authentic leadership and servant leadership. At the conclusion of the chapter, three cutting-edge issues in leadership that promise to be relevant in the 21st century were described—gender, culture, and emotions. These issues merit further study, as an understanding of their impact on leadership processes promises to enhance organizational practice.

TEACHING THE CHAPTER

At some time or another, your students have more than likely asked: What makes an effective leader? On playgrounds, one can observe the emergence of leadership in groups of children. Interestingly, such early perceptions are likely to influence how individuals view leaders and leadership throughout their lives. Many of your students may have recently participated in their very first presidential election. They probably asked themselves this question about effective leadership when deciding whom to vote into office. The question of leadership and the study of leaders are integral and significant parts of our society. Chapter 13 provides the opportunity for you to guide students through the numerous frameworks that have been offered to explain leadership emergence and effectiveness in organizations.

Your class will likely engage in lively discussion based on the content of this chapter. The exercises included below are aimed at getting students to think about their own experiences with leaders and what they expect from a leader when they are in a subordinate role. There is also a dark side to leadership, as it does not always result in positive, humanitarian outcomes. One question you may want to pose to your class is, "How do leaders get people to engage in bad behavior?" You may want to reference infamous leaders such as Hitler or Osama bin Laden. In addition, you may want to encourage debate about gender and leadership by splitting the class into groups of males and females and asking them to take the side of the other gender in the debate.

In the Web Learning section at the end of this chapter, a number of websites contain supplementary reading materials, including essays and recent news articles related to leadership. These sites include the Leader to Leader Institute, Fast Company, and Forbes.

SUGGESTED EXERCISES AND ASSIGNMENTS

What Is a Leader?

Purpose The objective of this exercise is to have students consider what stereotypes or assumptions they have about leaders and what makes them effective or ineffective.

Instructions

- Ask students to write down the first person who comes to mind when they hear the word *leader* (they can use a pseudonym if it is someone that other students might know or if they are uncomfortable sharing someone's name in class).
- Have students write down 10 words that they feel describe that person's leadership.
- When students are done, ask them to pair up with another student and discuss the person that they picked, as well as the 10 words they wrote down.
- Come together as a class and ask students to share some interesting examples.

Discussion Questions

- Are most of the examples of leaders good leaders or bad leaders? Why do you think that is?
- What are some common themes you noticed as people shared their 10 words? Do you think these can be considered the most important characteristics of leaders? Why or why not?
- We often forget that leadership is not always a formal designation. Are there any examples of people who demonstrated leadership even when they were not officially a leader?
- What are some aspects of leadership that did not come up in your discussion? Why might these qualities be overlooked when we talk about leadership?

What Leaders Have in Common

Purpose The objective of this exercise is to have students think about their experiences with leaders, identify the qualities that led them to be perceived as leaders, and consider whether such qualities would generalize to other situations.

Instructions

- Ask students to write down their answers to the following questions:
  - What qualities have the effective leaders in your life had in common?
  - Have any differences existed among those leaders?
  - Why do you think those leaders were different? Were there aspects of the context, organization, people, or job that required different leadership qualities?
- Divide up the class into small groups of six to eight students.
- Ask each group to generate a compilation of its members' responses to the above questions and to make sure that they provide the following three lists:
  - Qualities that generalize across most effective leaders in most situations

- Qualities that seem to be very situation-specific
- Situational characteristics that require different leadership qualities or skills

Discussion Questions

- What is more important for effective leadership—leader qualities/capabilities or situational characteristics?
- What experience have you had with leaders? Have they been mostly good or mostly poor? Why?
- Did the poor leadership you experienced still lead to positive outcomes?

What's Your Leadership Style?

Purpose This activity will help students demonstrate their own leadership behaviors and give them new ideas for how to influence others.

Instructions

- *Prior to class:* Purchase enough small plastic or paper cups so that you can divide students into groups of three or four and provide each group with approximately 20–30 cups. You should also have enough blindfolds so that each group can have one.
- Divide the students into groups, give them the cups, and ask them to set a goal for how high they can build a tower of cups. Write each team's goals on the board.
- Tell the students that each group will have one "follower," who will be blindfolded. The follower is the only individual who is allowed to touch the cups. The rest of the group will serve as "leaders" who must help guide the follower in building the cup tower.
- Give the students 20–30 minutes to work on their towers. Walk around and observe how the leaders interact with the follower.
- After time is up, ask each group whether they met or exceeded their goal. Spend some time debriefing by asking the followers how each of their leaders behaved.

Discussion Questions

- How much time did leaders focus on initiating-structure (task-oriented) behaviors? Were these helpful or harmful to your goals?
- How much time did leaders focus on consideration (relationship-oriented) behaviors? Were these helpful to your goals?
- What were some leadership behaviors that seemed to be particularly helpful or harmful?
- What have you learned about your own leadership style through this exercise?

Creating the Prototypical Leader

Purpose Students will consider their expectations of a leader across a variety of situations and think about how their experiences reflect their own traits. They will also consider prototypes of followers and their impact on leader effectiveness.

Instructions

- Divide the class into groups of three or four students.
- Instruct groups to create a leader prototype and a follower prototype based on their own expectations about leader qualities, follower qualities, and the behaviors in which both leader and follower should engage.
- Ask groups to present their prototypes to the rest of the class.

Discussion Questions

- How easy was it for your group to develop a leader prototype that everyone agreed on? A follower prototype?
- What influence did your own skills and abilities have when you were developing your leader and follower expectations?
- Across the class, how similar are the prototypes that were created?

Breaking Through the Glass Ceiling

Purpose Students will discuss the issues surrounding women in leadership roles.

Instructions

- Before discussing the role of gender and leadership in class, you may want to assign an article that presents some current statistics about the representation of women in corporate or government leadership roles. Note that www.catalyst.org has a plethora of research papers that report statistics about women in leadership in a clear, easy-to-read manner. Under "Topics," select "Women in Leadership."
- Alternatively, there may be a current event involving women in leadership that may be worthy of discussion. For example, Ginni Rometty (CEO of IBM), Mary Barra (CEO of General Motors Company), or Hillary Clinton (currently a candidate for U.S. president).
- After presenting the chapter material on gender and leadership, hold a class discussion in one of three ways:
  - Split the class solely by gender to form debate teams (it may be interesting to have them discuss the questions from the opposite gender's point of view).
  - Divide the class into small groups, split evenly by gender, and have them discuss gender and leadership.
  - Hold an open discussion/debate about gender and leadership with the entire class.
- Present students with the following questions, giving ample time between each question for thorough discussion:
  - Can you think of a well-known or famous woman who holds an important leadership position? In what industry does she work? Is this industry female-oriented or male-oriented?
  - How are women leaders portrayed in movies, books, and so on?
  - Are women unfairly underrepresented in leadership roles?

- Do you think women and men are held to different standards in order to attain promotions in organizations?
- Are expectations the same for male and female leaders?
- Do you think women make greater sacrifices than men in order to ascend the corporate ladder?
- How would you increase the number of women in leadership positions? Would men perceive these methods as fair?

Discussion Questions

- *If applicable:* Did arguing from the other gender's point of view affect your perspective on the issues?
- What idea was most likely to be implemented by your group to reduce gender inequity?
- Are men likely to feel unfairly treated by interventions designed to give women a better opportunity to achieve leadership positions?
- What, if any, effect do work–life programs (e.g., telecommuting) have on the career and leadership development of men and women?

Developing your Leadership Values

Purpose Students will have an opportunity to reflect on their own leadership skills and values.

Instructions

- Ask students to list 10 values they feel a good leader should have (e.g., integrity, competence, open-mindedness)
- Once students have their 10 values listed, ask them to put a star next to the three most important values.
- When students are done, ask them to think about a time when they had to be a leader. This does not necessarily have to be a formal leadership role; it can even be a time when they stood up for something, or when they served as a role model or mentor for someone else. Have them revisit their list of leadership values, and circle any that they believed they demonstrated during that experience. Were they exhibiting the values they believed are important? What about the three most important—how did they embody those values?

Discussion Questions

- What were some ways that you exhibited some of these values? What are some ways you missed opportunities to exhibit these values?
- What are some issues or difficulties that hindered your ability to demonstrate these values?
- What can you do to ensure that your leadership is in line with your values?
- How do these values match up with some of the research and theories you have read about? Do you see examples of some of the topics that were covered in the chapter in your own values?

EVALUATING "TAKING IT TO THE FIELD"

The Chapter 13 activity involves a game developer and manufacturer that has recently increased its staff. The company has also experienced an increase in turnover, which appears to be related to leadership. The owner, Sophie Konig, has read a trendy leadership book that provides weak advice for how to change her leadership style. Below are some suggestions for evaluating responses.

Poor responses...	▪ Provide a superficial response to the book's suggestions (e.g., "This sounds great!").
	▪ Indicate that the approach is not good but fail to clearly critique problems with the book's advice.
	▪ Fail to provide an additional suggestion for changing Sophie's leadership, or provide an approach that has little empirical support or limited applicability (e.g., Fiedler's contingency theory).
	▪ Provide an approach with research support but misunderstand or misapply the approach.
Good responses...	▪ Critique book's advice and clearly explain the problem:
	▪ The book claims that female leaders must be more aggressive, but research on the double bind suggests that aggressive women tend to be rated negatively.
	▪ The book's suggestion that she behave in a threatening way toward employees sounds a little like some of the behaviors associated with the dark triad.
	▪ The book suggests a response that is solely focused on initiating structure, with little attention to relationships.
	▪ This advice flies in the face of modern leadership theories such as transformational leadership, LMX, authentic leadership, and servant leadership.
	▪ Suggest an additional approach that has mixed empirical support (e.g., LMX theory) or fail to provide enough detail about the suggestion to demonstrate a strong understanding of how to apply the theory.
Excellent responses...	▪ Critique book's advice and clearly explain the problem:
	▪ The book claims that female leaders must be more aggressive, but research on the double bind suggests that aggressive women tend to be rated negatively.
	▪ The book's suggestion that she behave in a threatening way toward employees sounds a little like some of the behaviors associated with the dark triad.

■ The book suggests a response that is solely focused on initiating structure, with little attention to relationships.

■ This advice flies In the face of modern leadership theories such as transformational leadership, LMX, authentic leadership, and servant leadership.

■ Suggest an alternative approach with strong empirical support (e.g. transformational leadership theory) and provide enough detail to show a firm grasp of the key concepts. Excellent answers may point out ways that Sophie's approach is effective (e.g., getting to know employees as individuals, which aligns with individualized consideration) and suggest which pieces she may need to focus on (e.g., perhaps employees are not feeling inspired about their collective mission). Excellent responses may also point out that acting in an artificial way to go along with a book that doesn't have empirical support is a bad idea.

EVALUATING "APPLICATION QUESTIONS"

1. Consider each of the bases of power. How might a college instructor demonstrate each of these? How do you react when instructors use these types of power?

   Evaluation Guide: Students will likely come up with a variety of suggestions for this question. The following are common suggestions:

   ■ *Legitimate power:* Because instructors have a title and are considered to be in charge in the classroom, often just having a designation such as "professor" can lend them power.

   ■ *Reward power:* Instructors control course grades and points, so they have the ability to reward students for good work.

   ■ *Coercive power:* Instructors can also deduct points for poor performance, so they can use this basis of power to change student behavior.

   ■ *Expert power:* Instructors should be experts in their field, so students typically trust that what they say is true and accurate.

   ■ *Referent power:* Instructors who are excited about what they are teaching can emphasize the importance of learning to students. This is often important to students, as excitement can be contagious.

2. One aspect of LMX theory that researchers are beginning to explore is the varying quality of relationships within a team. Research demonstrates that when leaders have very strong relationships with only a few team members, it leads to turnover. Have you ever experienced something like this? Were you one of the favorites or one of the outsiders? What effect did this have on you?

Evaluation Guide: Most students will be able to come up with at least a few experiences of being an outsider or being a favorite. Some worthwhile points to make in this conversation include the following:

- Discuss with students how this affects their motivation. For example, if they are not a favorite, what can that do to their work ethic? It might be helpful to connect this discussion back to expectancy theory or organizational justice to show that many of these principles can apply to several areas of research.
- If you have students who were a favorite, ask them how it made them feel. Was it a pleasant experience, or was it uncomfortable? How did it affect their relationships with coworkers? Did they feel they deserved to be a favorite?
- Is it appropriate for a leader to show a preference for an employee who is a hard worker? What would transformational leadership have to say about this? What about transactional leadership?

3. Imagine you have a friend who is interested in becoming more transformational in her leadership style. What behaviors would you suggest she increase in order to become more transformational?

Evaluation Guide: Students can suggest a number of different ideas for how to become more transformational. It may be useful to discuss what they, personally, can do to be better leaders in their own lives. Here are some discussion points and examples:

- *Idealized influence and inspirational motivation:* Leaders who are passionate and excited about their work can help get workers excited as well. It is also important for leaders to "practice what they preach" so that they serve as a good role model for followers.
- *Intellectual stimulation:* Finding "stretch assignments" for followers can help people develop and become more creative. Students may also mention providing time and support for trying something new and making mistakes.
- *Individualized consideration:* Leaders should get to know their followers and know what sorts of goals and preferences they have. Taking time to connect with followers and provide developmental feedback can be key.

4. Consider some examples of famous female leaders. What are some ways in which female leaders are treated differently than male leaders (by the media as well as by peers and followers)?

Evaluation Guide: Students should be able to think of some prominent female leaders. Some students may get somewhat heated in this discussion, particularly if they feel that sexism and the glass ceiling are not issues. It may also be worth noting that, although liberals tend to be more outspoken about issues of sexism, female politicians from both the left and the right have experienced sexism. Some examples are listed below:

- *Hillary Clinton:* Particularly during her campaign for the Democratic presidential nomination, Clinton had to face a number of negative images in the media. She was often critiqued for being too tough and aggressive; however, after choking up during an interview, she began to be criticized for being too weak. A number of products mocked her toughness, such as a nutcracker designed to look like her.

- *Carly Fiorina:* Before Fiorina ran in the 2016 Republican primary, she had been outspoken about sexism she experienced in her position as CEO of Hewlett-Packard. In her book *Tough Choices*, she recounted that she once had to join her male colleagues at a strip club in order to meet an important client. She also said that while CEO, she was "referred to as a 'bimbo' or a 'bitch,' too soft or too hard, and presumptuous, besides." In 2015, while campaigning for the Republican presidential nomination, her rival Donald Trump said about her, "Look at that face! Would anyone vote for that?" Her rivals also often accused her of using her gender to gain an advantage with voters.
- *Condoleeza Rice:* The secretary of state under President George W. Bush, Rice often had to field questions in interviews about her marital status and whether she planned to have children. She also received widespread criticism when she wore an above-the-knee skirt with knee-high boots. In addition, in the wake of the 2011 Libyan rebellion, she discussed having awkward meetings with Muammar Gaddafi, who made several romantic overtures toward her.
- *Margaret Thatcher:* Called the Iron Lady for her toughness and her approach to the Soviet Union, Thatcher first assumed a position as Great Britain's secretary of state for education and science, and she had difficulty getting Prime Minister Edward Heath to listen to her suggestions (he seemed to consider her a token female whom he had to accept to appear inclusive). She was also asked many questions about whether she would have time to be a leader, given that she had children.
- A number of historical female leaders and political figures (e.g., Cleopatra, Anne Bolyn) often have their sexual exploits discussed as part of their rise to power, an aspect that is rarely discussed with male leaders.

5. Consider servant leadership. What might be some behaviors a leader could engage in that would indicate s/he was a servant leader? Why do you believe servant leadership is such a popular approach right now?

Evaluation Guide: Students should be able to identify some specific behaviors that would show that a leader is empowering, humble, authentic, accepting, guiding, and a good steward (e.g., not holding high potential employees back from other positions; serving as a mentor; being honest and upfront with others; balancing praise with constructive feedback; acting responsibly with a company's resources). Students also should be able to generate some ideas about why this theory has gained a foothold in the research and applied areas (e.g., people are less tolerant of corporate scandals and irresponsible leadership; this theory has a boost from the popularity of transformational leadership theory; the workplace is more focused on developing employees, so this type of leader would support a development environment).

HIGHLIGHTED STUDY FOR DISCUSSION

Falbe, C. M., & Yukl, G. (1992). Consequences for managers of using single influence tactics and combinations of tactics. *Academy of Management Journal, 35*, 638–652.

Although the textbook does not discuss influence tactics, they are strongly related to leadership and how people respond to the influence attempts of others. The main points of the article are as follows:

- The researchers examined three outcomes of an influence attempt: resistance (where the individual refuses to comply with a request), compliance (where the individual carries out a task but shows no initiative or engagement), and commitment (where an individual carries out a request enthusiastically and willingly).
- The researchers also examined the following influence tactics:
    - Inspirational appeals (where the requester appeals to the target's values)
    - Consultation (where the requester seeks the target's help in completing a task)
    - Rational persuasion (where the requester attempts to persuade the target by using facts, statistics, or logical arguments)
    - Ingratiation (where the requester uses flattery or similar behaviors to influence the target)
    - Personal appeals (where the requester appeals to the target's feelings of friendship)
    - Exchange (where the requester offers to trade favors for the target's cooperation)
    - Pressure (where the requester uses threats or demands to get what he or she wants)
    - Legitimating (where the requester uses his or her authority or rules to influence others)
    - Coalition (where the requester enlists endorsements from others to persuade the target)
- Researchers asked MBA students to provide critical incidents describing a time when someone tried to influence them, as well as their response to the tactic. These qualitative responses were coded by researchers.
- The results indicated that rational persuasion was the most common tactic used but succeeded in gaining commitment in only 23% of cases. Inspirational appeals, although rarely used, gained commitment in 90% of cases. Legitimating was best for gaining compliance. Coalition and pressure typically resulted in high rates of resistance.
- The researchers also compared "soft" techniques (ingratiation, consultation, inspirational appeals, and personal appeals) with "hard" techniques (pressure, legitimating, and coalition) and rational persuasion. Results indicated commitment was most likely when an individual used a combination of soft techniques or combined a soft technique with rational persuasion. Using a combination of hard techniques was most likely to result in resistance or compliance.

WEB LEARNING

Title	Address
The Leader to Leader Institute: An extension of the Drucker Foundation	http://www.druckerinstitute.com/monday/
Center for Creative Leadership	http://www.ccl.org/Leadership/index.aspx
ChangingMinds.org: Leadership Theories	http://changingminds.org/disciplines/leadership/theories/leadership_theories.htm
Circles USA	http://www.circlesusa.org/
Big Dog & Little Dog: The Art and Science of Leadership	http://www.nwlink.com/~Donclark/leader/leader.html
Forbes magazine: Leadership page	http://www.forbes.com/leadership
Fast Company: Leadership page	http://www.fastcompany.com/section/leadership-now
Catalyst: Research on women in leadership roles (Go to the Knowledge Center, under "Topics" select "Women in Leadership")	http://www.catalyst.org
Leadership Learning Community	http://leadershiplearning.org/
The Institute for Management Excellence	http://www.itstime.com

CHAPTER 14

Organizational Theory and Development

LEARNING OBJECTIVES

This chapter should help students understand:

- The various organizational theories and how they have developed
- The differences between bureaucratic theory and Scientific Management
- How Theory X differs from Theory Y
- How open-system theory provides a useful framework for thinking about organizations
- What organizational development is and why it is so important for the long-term success of organizations
- The basic premises on which organizational change is based
- The major principles of many organizational development interventions, as well as some benefits of each
- Some of the specifics concerning organizational development interventions, such as total quality management and gainsharing
- Technostructural interventions such as reengineering
- How culture-change interventions and knowledge-management interventions can act to transform organizations profoundly

Chapter Summary

This chapter presents information about two related organizational topics: organizational theory and organizational development. These were defined and discussed in terms of their importance to the effectiveness of organizations. I then presented three organizational theories: classical organizational theory, with its emphasis on Scientific Management and bureaucracy, and the more recent approaches known as humanistic theory and open-system theory.

Before discussing various techniques of organizational development, I spent considerable time highlighting reasons why companies, if they are to be successful, must pursue OD. I also presented examples of companies that have succeeded in part because of OD, as well as examples of companies that did not succeed owing to a lack of flexibility and willingness to change. In this context, I provided a detailed discussion of Lewin's general change model and the more well-developed action research model.

Next, I considered some of the most frequently used OD interventions, such as survey feedback, team building, total quality management, and gainsharing; empirical support was cited, along with a description of their potential benefits and disadvantages. I also introduced more recently conceived OD interventions such as reengineering, information technology, and appreciative inquiry. Finally, I discussed organizational transformation in the context of interventions that profoundly change the nature of the organization. Here, I discussed the role of culture change and knowledge management specifically as determinants of organizational innovation.

TEACHING THE CHAPTER

Chapter 14 is devoted solely to the "O side" of I/O psychology. While previous chapters (e.g., Chapter 9—Motivation) covered primarily "O-side" topics, this chapter examines the organization as a whole by presenting material focused on organizational theory and organizational development. Something to keep in mind and share with students is how this theoretical work fits into a historical context. Specifically, Frederick Taylor's theorizing and ideas about Scientific Management were developed during the industrial revolution, when organizations and management were struggling with how to manage people and machines. After World War II, humanistic theories were developed in response to a rapidly growing population, industrial strength, and the emergence of a service economy. For the first time, employees began considering work as more than just a paycheck, growing sensitive to how organizations affected their lives outside the workplace. With the growth and expansion of modern-day organizations, more sophisticated theories, such as open-system theory, have emerged to help explain organizational production and coordination.

During the last 25 years, the management consulting industry has grown rapidly in response to organizational change and development. Again, the historical context should not be ignored and may supplement class material very well. In the early 1980s, American industry experienced difficult times due to increasing competition from Japanese products and industry. After creating a competitive advantage for the Japanese, total quality management (TQM) practices emerged in the United States by the mid-1980s to improve the product quality and market share of American goods. Today, quality is still an important performance criterion for organizations and is heavily emphasized across industries. Several of the websites listed at the end of the chapter can provide students with further information relating to TQM and other popular organizational development tools such as team building and gainsharing.

Additionally, below is a list of resources you may want to consider for team-building and organizational development activities that may be fun yet educational for your class. This is not meant to be an endorsement of these books; this list is *only* for information-sharing purposes.

Harrington-Mackin, D. (2007). *The team-building tool kit: Tips and tactics for effective workplace teams.* New York: AMACOM.

Miller, B. C. (2003). *Quick team-building activities for busy managers: 50 exercises that get results in 15 minutes.* New York: AMACOM.

Newstrom, J. W. (2008). *The big book of team-building: Quick, fun activities for building morale, communication, and team spirit.* New York: McGraw-Hill.

Senge, P. M., Kleiner, A., Roberts, C., Ross, R., & Smith, B. (1994). *The fifth discipline fieldbook.* New York: Crown Publishing.

Sikes, S. W. (1995). *Feeding the zircon gorilla and other team building activities.* Tulsa, OK: Learning Unlimited Corporation.

Sikes, S. W. (1998). *Executive marbles and other team building activities.* Tulsa, OK: Learning Unlimited Corporation.

SUGGESTED EXERCISES AND ASSIGNMENTS

Theory X Versus Theory Y

Purpose Students will consider how they think about organizational work and reflect on how their ideas might have changed over the course of the semester.

Instructions

- Find or design a measure to assess whether students tend to agree with Theory Y or Theory X philosophies (you can find an example at http://www.proprofs.com/quiz-school/story.php?title=are-you-theory-x-manager-theory-y-manager).
- Provide students with their scores (or ask students to score the measure on their own).

Discussion Questions

- Did you find you agreed more with Theory X or Theory Y? What experiences have led you to believe this?
- Do you believe your philosophy has changed over the course of this class? How?
- What are some topics we've talked about in class so far that seem to support the importance of Theory Y?

Overcoming Personal Roadblocks to Success

Purpose Students will simulate business process reengineering relating to their own academic performance via brainstorming and problem solving.

Instructions

- This exercise will likely be covered as students start to think about the end of the semester and final exams. This exercise offers them the opportunity to consider their performance, their satisfaction with that performance, and what they might have done to perform better.

■ Ask students to think about their performance in this class throughout the semester. Instruct students to individually answer the following questions:

■ To what extent are you satisfied with your overall performance?

■ What factors acted as roadblocks for you? Specifically, what factors got in the way of achieving better performance? If no roadblocks were encountered, what factors were overcome in order to achieve successful performance in this class?

■ Considering this list of factors, rate each factor (yes/no) on whether it was *within* your control or *outside of* your control.

■ For factors within your control, what could you have done to deal with them more effectively?

■ On a scale of 1 (very easy) to 5 (very hard), how difficult would it be to make these changes? For factors outside of your control, what could you have done to minimize their effects on successful performance in class?

■ You might want to consider using this example as a template for students:

Roadblock	Within Your Control	Change Strategy	Difficulty of Change
Attended too many parties	Yes	Attend fewer weeknight parties	4

■ Divide the class into groups of four to six students to discuss their roadblocks and strategies for change.

■ Instruct each group to develop a list of their top roadblocks and their plans for change. Then have each group present their ideas to the rest of the class.

Discussion Questions

■ Will you be able to implement these change strategies in your future classes? Why or why not?

■ Were you surprised by the number of roadblocks you identified?

■ Were there any surprising roadblocks?

■ What was the roadblock that was most difficult to change among your group?

Organizational Development and Management Fads

Purpose The objective of this exercise is to familiarize students with different commercially available interventions and help them understand how they fit into the general types of interventions.

Instructions

■ If computers with Internet access are available, this activity can be done in class. If not, during the previous class you can ask students to do some research before the next class session.

- Ask groups of students to gather basic information about trendy (or formerly trendy) interventions. Some examples might include the following:
  - ISO 9000
  - Theory Z
  - Six Sigma
  - Kaizen
  - Knowledge management
  - Quality circles
  - One-Minute Management
  - Reengineering
  - Matrix management
- Have students present their information to one another (either in front of everyone, or create new groups that have one representative from each group).

Discussion Questions
- Do you believe any of these interventions are fads? Why?
- What is the difference (if any) between organizational development and management fads?
- What skills or knowledge would someone need to identify a fad?
- How might you test these interventions to determine if they are actually effective?

Creating Culture Change

Purpose Students will consider what is involved in changing the culture, even within a small organization.

Instructions
- Ask students to spend a few minutes thinking of a way to describe a culture they are part of (e.g., your college/university or your classroom).
- Have students share some of their thoughts, and then ask them how they might change the culture (e.g., if the classroom is typically quiet, ask them how they might change it into a place where people speak up more).
- Have students work in pairs or groups to devise ways in which the culture of the classroom could change.
- Have students share their ideas.

Discussion Questions
- Do you think culture change here is possible? Why or why not?
- Which of these suggestions do you think would be most successful? Why?
- What are some barriers to culture change you can think of?

Organizational Development Interventionist for a Day

Purpose Students will consider the various types of organizational development (OD) interventions and apply them to an organizational scenario.

Instructions

- *Prior to class:* You might want to have copies of the following scenario available for each student/group:

You are an organizational development consultant at RPJ Consulting, Inc. You have just been hired by the CompuCool company, which designs and sells "netbooks" (small laptop computers with limited capability that cost less than $300). In the past year, the company has gone from 150 employees with virtually no organizational chart to 1,500 employees working in the areas of research and development, production, sales, marketing, and finance.

CompuCool primarily manufactures netbooks, but it also produces small accessories for the netbook (e.g., case, wireless mouse, etc.). The company's sales have gone from $3 million to $15 million in two years. Furthermore, the founders of the company were college roommates, are very laid back, and do not like a lot of rules and procedures. To this point, the company culture has been very informal, with few procedures in place. CompuCool's mission statement, which has existed since the beginning of the company, reads, "Our mission is to produce a cool, accessible netbook computer for all people. In doing so, we want to have fun while making a difference and maybe a profit, too." The company has hired you because they are concerned with the company's overall effectiveness, efficiency, and productivity.

- Divide the class into groups of four to six.
- Instruct the groups to address the following:
  - How would you go about diagnosing CompuCool's problems? What appear to be the main organizational problems?
  - Choose two OD interventions to implement to help the organization achieve its goals. Describe why you chose these methods and draw up detailed plans for how you will go about addressing the OD issues in the organization.
  - What obstacles might you face in implementing these interventions?
  - Who would you involve in your planning?
  - How would you get the two company founders to support your ideas?

Discussion Questions

- How difficult was it to select interventions for this situation?
- To what extent do you believe it would be difficult to conduct an OD intervention in this situation?
- How would you determine if your intervention was effective?
- Have you ever participated in an activity that was part of an OD intervention?

EVALUATING "TAKING IT TO THE FIELD"

In the Chapter 14 activity, the CEO of a software company is asking for help implementing a knowledge management system in his company. He has outlined several problems and asked students to explain what knowledge management is, what tools he would need to implement this, and specific steps he could take to implement the change. Responses will vary, particularly depending upon whether your students have taken a research methods class prior to your class. Their responses may also vary depending upon how in-depth you have covered information about measurement and surveying in your class. However, a rough guideline to grading is provided below.

Poor responses...	<ul><li>Fail to define knowledge management and connect the value of this concept to the needs of a software company.</li><li>Provide only basic tools for knowledge management that are likely to be too static to be useful to a software company (e.g., libraries, training for new employees).</li><li>Fail to provide clear steps for how to craft the knowledge management system.</li><li>Fail to discuss steps the CEO should take to ensure the success of the intervention.</li></ul>
Good responses...	<ul><li>Define knowledge management and emphasize its value for a software company that requires continuous learning among its employees.</li><li>Provide suggestions for tools that might help employees stay up to date on software (e.g., online trainings, discussion boards).</li><li>Provide specific steps the organization can take to determine how to craft these materials (e.g., soliciting feedback from employees).</li><li>Suggest specific steps the CEO can take to ensure success with a culture change (e.g., having upper management express commitment to continuous learning, rewarding employees for staying up to date on materials).</li></ul>
Excellent responses...	<ul><li>Define knowledge management and emphasize its value for a software company that requires continuous learning among its employees.</li><li>Provide creative suggestions for tools that might help employees stay up to date on software (e.g., online trainings, discussion boards that crowdsource solutions, social media tools).</li><li>Provide specific steps the organization can take to determine how to craft these materials (e.g., soliciting feedback from employees, pilot testing tools).</li><li>Suggest specific steps the CEO can take to ensure success with a culture change (e.g., having upper management express commitment to continuous learning, rewarding employees for staying up-to-date on materials). May also emphasize important new positions that should be in place (e.g., establishing a chief knowledge officer).</li></ul>

EVALUATING "APPLICATION QUESTIONS"

1. Think of a time you had had to deal with a bureaucracy. What did you need to do? Did you see any reason for that bureaucracy's existence?

   Evaluation Guide: Most students will have experienced some level of bureaucracy. For example, students will commonly express irritation at paperwork they have to fill out for the university/college. This discussion might help clarify the difference between useful and wasteful bureaucracy, and how this can change over time. The following may be helpful points to make:

   - Sometimes bureaucracy is important and necessary. For example, students who are taking a course abroad may need to provide a great deal of paperwork for their own safety.
   - Sometimes bureaucracy was once important but has now outlived its usefulness. For example, if an administrative assistant requires hard copies of documents that are available online, this would be an example of a bureaucracy that has not appropriately adapted to technology.
   - Sometimes bureaucracy is created needlessly because the individual making the decision did not realize the amount of work he or she was creating. For example, if a higher-up official decides to change a form so that it now requires two departments to collaborate to fill it out, rather than having separate documents that each department can fill out independently, that official may have unknowingly created a need for additional meetings between the departments.

2. Have you ever been in an organization that was undergoing an organizational development intervention? What happened? How did employees react?

   Evaluation Guide: Some students may not have had any experience in organizations that were experiencing major changes, so even discussing minor procedural changes (e.g., a new sandwich on a menu) can provide them with an idea of what that situation is like. Some points worth making are listed below:

   - Frequency of organizational change is important. In organizations where there are always new changes in progress, employees can become jaded, especially when the changes fail to produce meaningful and practical outcomes.
   - Communication is important as well; interventions that are not supported by upper management and that are not well explained and justified also tend to fail.

3. Consider an organization where you have worked. Do you think this organization was a "learning organization"? Why or why not?

   Evaluation Guide: Students will have a wide variety of experience on this topic. Some students might have worked in relatively low-level jobs in organizations that tend to promote from within (e.g., Starbuck's, Target, the U.S. military); others might have worked in smaller organizations where entry-level jobs rarely develop into lifelong careers. Below are some points to discuss:

- Learning organizations have a number of benefits. Workers are more likely to stay loyal to the company if they feel they can develop and grow their career there. Workers also may enjoy learning and feel valued if they are compensated for spending extra time learning relevant information. Some organizations may also support employees who go back to school to earn degrees that are relevant to the company.

- Learning organizations also face some difficulties. Workers will sometimes need to be away from work or decrease their workload to engage in these learning activities (employees are unlikely to be willing to use their personal time to take a training course, so someone will need to cover for them while they are gone). Furthermore, if the organization makes continuous learning a requirement, individuals who are not interested in learning more may end up leaving or being fired, which could be a problem.

- In general, most students appreciate a company that supports continuous learning, so discussing their experiences in such an environment will help them understand how common such an appreciation is and some of the ways they were able to develop in the workplace.

4. Consider positive organizational development. Do you believe people should spend more time focusing on using their strengths or addressing their weaknesses? Why?

Evaluation Guide: This is an ongoing controversy in the I/O arena, and students may have strong opinions about this. Here are some points in the debate worth noting:

- Focusing on strengths rather than weaknesses seems inclusive because it assumes everyone has a strength. It also is thought to help people feel more empowered in their work. A number of measures (e.g., StrengthsFinder) focus on finding strengths and leveraging them, and employees seem to like this approach.

- Focusing only on strengths, however, may allow individuals to overlook weaknesses that are actively harming their performance. Some also argue that focusing on strengths removes accountability for some individuals, which can be problematic.

5. Imagine you work for a company that uses gainsharing. Do you think you would like it? Why or why not?

Evaluation Guide: Most students will initially be in favor of gainsharing. In order to generate more discussion, consider splitting the class into a debate of pro versus con, or ask the following questions:

- Think about group projects you have worked on where all members received the same number of points. What were some things you found frustrating about that situation?

- Think about what types of rewards you would prefer: Stocks? Cash? An upgrade to a better office? A group vacation? Keeping in mind that everyone has to receive the same reward, which would you suggest companies use for their reward system?

■ How would you solicit employee suggestions for gainsharing, and how would you encourage them to continue to share their ideas in the long run?

HIGHLIGHTED STUDY FOR DISCUSSION

Vermeulen, F., Puranam, P., & Gulati, R. (2010). Change for change's sake. *Harvard Business Review, 88,* 70–76.

This article, from the *Harvard Business Review,* provides an interesting opportunity to discuss the importance of empirical support in OD. The main points of the article are as follows:

■ The authors make the case that even untroubled organizations should engage in organizational change from time to time. They argue that organizations that are doing well tend to overlook inefficiencies, routines, and silos that have developed over time.

■ First, the authors suggest reorienting the organization around a new criterion. They provide the example of Cisco Systems, which created a centralized R&D group to facilitate technical innovation. It may be useful to ask students whether they think this change would work for all organizations and what might prompt an organization to do this.

■ Second, the authors suggest that being proactive in changing can help break up routines and typical ways of doing work. They cite GE Healthcare, which changed the organizational structure and created new positions intended to reconnect equipment and service silos. This provides an opportunity to ask students about some of the implications of changing the organizational structure, which are downplayed by the authors.

■ Third, the authors suggest that groups within an organization can become too powerful over time and that resource allocation is not done properly. They cite Jones Lang LaSalle, where a new CEO broke up the three divisions and integrated them. The authors note that senior executives left when they lost their power and influence but that the change eliminated bottlenecks. Asking students to consider what research in I/O might say about this change will help them think critically about the change.

■ The article also provides a small test that the authors suggest be handed out to managers to assess whether it is time for a change. This would provide a good opportunity for students to consider and discuss test development and validation. It also might be helpful to discuss what it would mean if managers or CEOs make decisions based on the outcomes of this measure.

WEB LEARNING

Title	Address
American Society for Quality (ASQ)	http://asq.org/index.aspx
Baldrige Performance Excellence Program	http://www.nist.gov/baldrige/
The W. Edwards Deming Institute	https://deming.org/
HR Guide: Compensation, Incentive Plans, Gainsharing	http://www.hr-guide.com/data/G443.htm
The Fifth Discipline Field Book Project	http://www.gurteen.com/gurteen/gurteen.nsf/id/fifth-discipline-field-book
Organizational Development Network	http://www.odnetwork.org/
Action Science Network	http://www.actionscience.com
Change Management Toolbook	http://www.change-management-toolbook.com/
Open Systems Theory	http://faculty.babson.edu/krollag/org_site/encyclop/open_system.html
Academy of Management: Organization and Management Theory	http://omtweb.org/
Peter Senge and the Learning Organization	http://infed.org/mobi/peter-senge-and-the-learning-organization/
Free Management Library: Team Building	http://managementhelp.org/groups/team-building.htm